concerning who was responsible for Sardius's death (Ira Glaze, William Reynolds, Stephen Reynolds, or Jesse Maupin).

Warren Smith—Mortally wounded while in the blacksmith shop. He died shortly after the Missourians stormed the building.

John York—Mortally wounded while trying to escape from the blacksmith shop. He was reported to have been shot in the head and died the day after the attack.

WOUNDED

Jacob Foutz—Wounded in the thigh while in the blacksmith shop and escaped being killed by pretending to be dead.

Jacob Hawn—Founder of the mill and the Hawn's Mill community. Wounded while trying to escape from the blacksmith shop.

Charles Jimison [Jameson]—Wounded while trying to escape from the blacksmith shop.

Nathan K. Knight—Wounded in the attack. While yelling for quarters his finger was shot off and another finger was injured. In making his escape he was wounded in his leg and back.

Isaac Leany—Wounded in ten places while trying to escape from the blacksmith shop. Four balls passed entirely through his body (leaving eight holes). He was also grazed by two more bullets, resulting in flesh wounds to each arm. He lived thirty-five years to the day of the massacre.

Tarlton Lewis—Wounded in the shoulder while trying to escape from the blacksmith shop.

Gilmon Merrill—Wounded while trying to escape from the blacksmith shop.

George Myers—Wounded in the right shoulder while trying to escape from the blacksmith shop. He lived a little more than a mile from the mill. After receiving his injury he crawled back to his home. He never fully recovered from his injury.

Jacob Myers Jr.—Wounded while trying to escape from the blacksmith shop. His leg was broken by a bullet that lodged halfway between his knee and ankle. He also received a flesh wound to the thigh. He lived near the mill and assisted in running it. A year after the attack, his leg was amputated due to his injuries.

Jacob Potts—Wounded twice in the right leg while trying to escape from the blacksmith shop.

Hiram Rathbun—Wounded in his right leg shortly after the attack on the settlement began. He remained crippled for the rest of his life. He later joined the Reorganized Church of Jesus Christ of Latter Day Saints.

Alma Smith—Mormon boy, age six, son of Warren and Amanda B. Smith. Alma went into the blacksmith shop at the time of the attack and hid behind the bellows. While hiding, a Missourian saw him from between the cracks and deliberately shot him at close range, wounding him in the hip. He fully recovered from the injury.

Mary Stedwell—Wounded in the hand while trying to escape as the attack began.

John Walker—Wounded in his right arm while in the blacksmith shop. He and his family lived about five miles from the mill.

William Yokum—Wounded in the face and leg while trying to escape from the blacksmith shop. His leg was later amputated.

Tragedy and Truth: What Happened at
Hawn's Mill

General Editor, Alexander L. Baugh

Contributing Editors, Glenn Rawson and Dennis Lyman

Contributions by Max H Parkin, Gerrit Dirkmaat, and Brent M. Rogers

Covenant Communications, Inc.

Cover images—Top image: *Haun's Mill* © Al Rounds; for more information, visit www.alrounds.com. **Bottom Left:** *I'll Never Forsake* © Julie Rogers; for more information, visit www.julierogersart.com. **Bottom Middle:** *Sardius Smith* © AD Shaw. **Bottom Right:** *Staging the Attack* © Kelly Donovan. **Front Flap:** *Gallatin Brawl* by Kelly Donovan. **Back Flap:** *The Attack* by Kelly Donovan. **Back Cover:** *Hawn's Mill and Blacksmith Shop* © Kirt Harmon; for more information, visit www.harmonartonline.com.

Cover and interior design copyright © 2014 by Covenant Communications, Inc.

Published by Covenant Communications, Inc.
American Fork, Utah

Copyright © 2014 by Glenn Rawson, Dennis Lyman, Alexander L. Baugh, Max H Parkin, Gerrit Dirkmaat, and Brent M. Rogers.

All rights reserved. No part of this book may be reproduced in any format or in any medium without the written permission of the publisher, Covenant Communications, Inc., P. O. Box 416, American Fork, UT 84003. This work is not an official publication of The Church of Jesus Christ of Latter-day Saints. The views expressed within this work are the sole responsibility of the author and do not necessarily reflect the position of The Church of Jesus Christ of Latter-day Saints, Covenant Communications, Inc., or any other entity.

Printed in China
First Printing: October 2014

20 19 18 17 16 15 14   10 9 8 7 6 5 4 3 2 1

ISBN 978-1-62108-840-0

Table of Contents

Mormonism on Missouri's Western Frontier, 1830-1838 1

The 1838 Mormon-Missouri War:
Historical Setting to the Hawn's Mill Tragedy 29

Jacob Hawn and the Hawn's Mill Settlement in Eastern Caldwell County . . . 57

A Scene of Blood and Horror:
The Attack on the Hawn's Mill Settlement 77

Living with the Memory of the Hawn's Mill Massacre:
Aftermath, Exodus, and Efforts to Obtain Redress 105

Mormonism on Missouri's Western Frontier, 1830–1838

Max H Parkin

MISSION TO THE LAMANITES

The drama of the Mormons in Missouri began on January 13, 1831, when five missionaries—including Oliver Cowdery, Peter Whitmer Jr., Parley P. Pratt, Richard Ziba Peterson, and Frederick G. Williams, an Ohio convert—arrived in Independence, Missouri, a rough-hewn village and seat of Jackson County, situated on the edge of America's frontier, ten miles from the state's western boundary.[1] In an 1830 revelation, the Prophet named the state boundary "on the borders of the Lamanites," which the missionaries would soon cross to begin teaching the Indians.[2] Cowdery, the group's leader, noted that they had been sent west to "rear up a pillar as a witness where the temple of God shall be built, in the glorious new Jerusalem."[3] Later that summer, Joseph Smith himself would arrive and designate Jackson County as the land of Zion, and a site immediately west of Independence as the location for the temple.

The missionaries arrived at Independence after having traveled the last three hundred miles on foot in the dead of winter. Parley Pratt recalled that the biting cold wind blew with such keenness it would "almost take the skin off the face."[4] The inclement season was so remarkably cold and snowy that it became known by the settlers as the "winter of the deep snow."[5]

In May 1830, seven months before the arrival of the missionaries, Congress passed the Indian Removal Act, signed by President Andrew Jackson, establishing the region west of Missouri and Arkansas as Indian Territory.[6] In the area just west of Jackson County and south of the Kansas River, the Shawnees, a peaceful farming tribe, had been settling for nearly two years. However, because of the difficult winter conditions, the Delaware Indians, who had been living in southern Indiana since 1821, and their leader of white and Indian ancestry—

The first Latter-day Saints in Missouri were a group of missionaries led by Oliver Cowdery that had been called by revelation (see D&C 32) and sent west "into the wilderness among the Lamanites."

Chief Kikthawenund (sometimes referred to as Kithilhund, but also known as William Anderson)—had only begun arriving on their land just north of the Kansas River and were in a precarious and unsettled condition when the Mormon missionaries arrived.[7]

Upon arriving in Indian Territory, Cowdery, Pratt, and Williams went first to a nearby Shawnee village and "tarried one night," wrote Pratt.[8] The following day they crossed the Kansas River to visit the Delawares and met Chief William Anderson, "an aged and venerable looking man, who had long stood at the head of the Delawares."[9]

At first, the chief hesitated to listen to the missionaries until being informed about the Book of Mormon, which increased his interest. The following day he established a council with forty of his men to be instructed at length by Cowdery, who again spoke about the Book of Mormon. Their talks continued "for several days," and the missionaries received assurance that in the spring Chief Anderson would build a council house for the missionaries to more completely teach about their religion.[10]

Indian agent Richard W. Cummins, however, objected to the missionaries being on the Indian lands without a government permit. Peter Whitmer Jr. reported that Cummins threatened the Mormon elders with imprisonment at the cantonment if they continued preaching.[11] Alarmed, Cowdery wrote to General William Clark, Superintendent of Indian Affairs at St. Louis, for "a permit for myself"

U.S. President Andrew Jackson designated the region west of Missouri as Indian lands. It was into this area that the missionaries traveled and preached.

Oliver Cowdery and his companions had little success preaching to the Indians until they taught about the Book of Mormon. Its message captured the interest of the Indians.

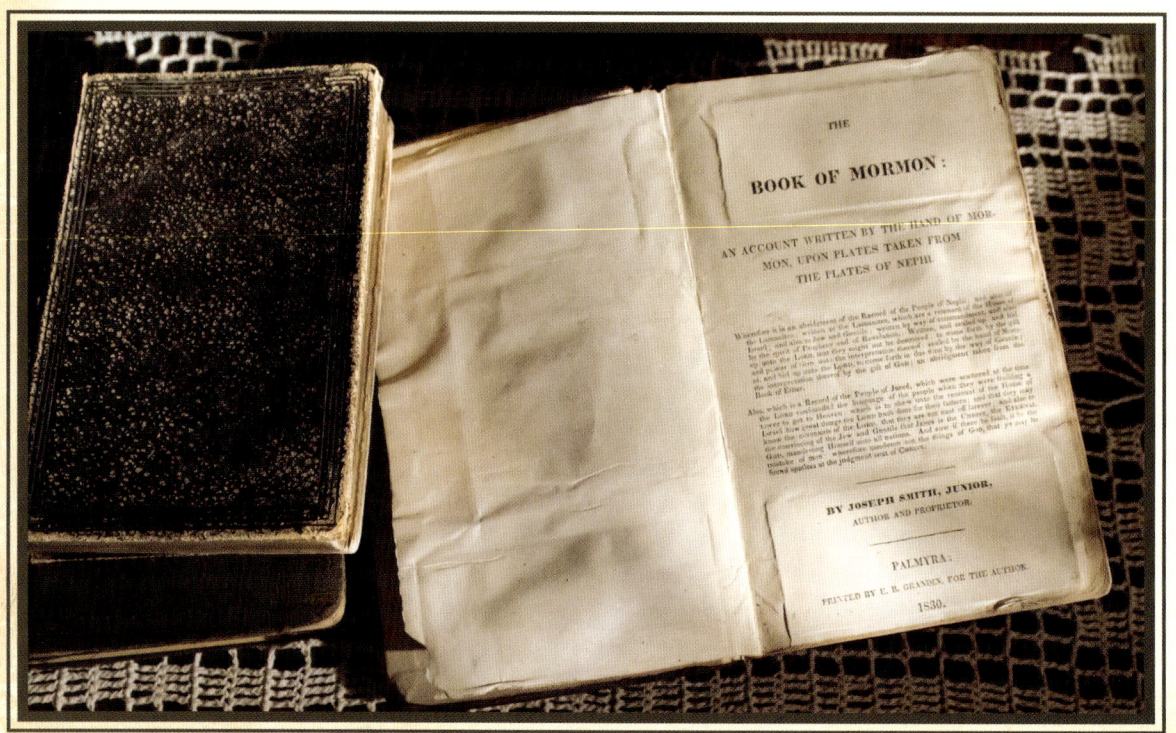

Top: Andrew Jackson, courtesy of the Library of Congress. Bottom: Book of Mormon Title Page © History of the Saints

and others to establish schools and teach the "several tribes."[12] Cummins also wrote to the superintendent: "A few days ago three men all strangers to me went among the Indians preaching. . . . I have refused to let them stay unless they first obtain permission from you."[13] Pratt traveled to St. Louis in February to see the superintendent, but Clark was away from his post and did not respond to Cowdery's request.[14] Unable to get a permit, Pratt declared, "Thus ended our first Indian Mission."[15]

That winter, their missionary work continued in Jackson County and in the spring eastward into Lafayette County. While the elders "taught school and tailored for our support," wrote Peter Whitmer Jr., they baptized seven.[16] Among those converted were Joshua Lewis and his family. Lewis resided eight miles west of Independence in Kaw Township, west of the Big Blue River. The Lewis house, a two-story log structure located near the Santa Fe Trail road that went west from Independence to the Indian agency and southward, was the place where early Mormons sometimes gathered, where Sidney Rigdon would dedicate the land of Zion, and where Church leaders would hold the first Missouri conference later that summer.[17] In April in Lafayette County, situated east of Jackson County, Oliver Cowdery and Richard Ziba Peterson baptized several converts, including Rebecca Hopper, whom Peterson married in August.[18]

General William Clark served as the Superintendent of Indian Affairs at St. Louis from 1822 to 1838. He is the same William Clark who had traveled with Meriwether Lewis on the Lewis and Clark Expedition to the West from 1803 to 1806. It was to him that the Mormon Missionaries appealed for permission to continue preaching to the Indians.

During their missionary efforts in Jackson County, Oliver Cowdery complained of unpleasant treatment by his neighbors. "We are greatly wondered at," he wrote from Kaw Township in April. A month later, with misgivings, he reported to his brethren in Ohio that "almost the whole country which consists of Universalists, Atheists, Deists, Presbyterians, Methodists, Baptists and other professed Christians, priests and people" are "united and foaming" against us. He added, disparagingly, "We dwell in the midst of scorpions."[19]

John Mason Peck, a Methodist circuit rider and early associate of Isaac McCoy, who spent forty years observing the advancing frontiers in the valleys of the Ohio and Missouri rivers, named three types of settlers in the West—illiterate backwoodsmen, disgruntled farmers, and enterprising men of capital and ambition. Each class had within it the orderly and the restless, which often included the unchurched, the intemperate, the lazy, and the lawless.[20] Moreover, at the time the Mormons were in Jackson County, Independence was the outfitting station for merchants who sent wares and supplies to Santa Fe, as well as trappers, Indian traders, and frontiersmen headed to the Far West.[21] A visitor who had traveled the country widely lamented that

"Independence was the roughest town he had ever seen, . . . [with] drinking, swearing and fighting."[22] The soon-arriving Mormons, mostly from New England, New York, Pennsylvania, and Ohio, observed a different culture than they had known in the Northeast. New Yorker William W. Phelps, upon arriving at Independence with Joseph Smith in July 1831, wrote, "The people are proverbially idle or lazy, and mostly ignorant." Because these Missourians came primarily from the South, Phelps noted that they came "with customs, manners, modes of living and a climate entirely different from the northerners."[23] John C. McCoy, Reverend Isaac McCoy's son and assistant surveyor, said that the differences between the settlers and the Mormons were so stark that it made them "completely unfitted to live together in peace and friendship" and "as wide apart as the poles."[24] It was among this society that the Mormons planned to build their Zion.

Oliver Cowdery wrote a letter to his brethren in Kirtland and detailed the persecution the Saints had received at the hands of Jackson County citizens. Jackson County in 1831 was the wild frontier and attracted a rough and ill-mannered ilk of men.

ESTABLISHING ZION

In February 1831, Joseph Smith moved to Kirtland, Ohio, and quickly gave his attention to four emerging concerns: (1) providing a financial means to build Zion, (2) identifying the exact site for the New Jerusalem, (3) publishing his revelations, and (4) establishing a body of the Church in Jackson County.

An early 1831 revelation to Joseph Smith set forth the financial law for the Church—a cooperative system of industry and disciplined living associated with the principles of consecration and stewardship. Church members who moved to Missouri were expected to transfer their temporal assets to the newly appointed bishop, Edward Partridge, and in turn receive a stewardship deed, usually a land grant or the means to operate a trade shop or mill. With these "inheritances," the stewards were expected to generate a surplus that would be used to establish the city of Zion and help the poor.²⁵ Church leaders subsequently established a literary firm, approved the Prophet's revelations for publication, purchased a press, and established a printing operation at Independence.²⁶

Joseph Smith, arriving at Independence, Missouri, July 14, 1831, "looked out the country and found the place for the City and Temple," wrote Joseph Knight Sr.²⁷ The city "should be called Zion," said Joseph Smith, "because it is to be a place of righteousness."²⁸ Independence was to be the "center place," stated a revelation, and "a spot for the temple is lying westward, upon a lot which is not far from the courthouse," just outside the town boundary.²⁹ "Independence," wrote Ezra Booth, an elder who arrived with Joseph Smith, was "a new town, containing a court-house built of brick, two or three merchant's stores, and 15 or 20 dwelling houses, built mostly of logs."³⁰ In time, the two communities—Independence and the New Jerusalem, in close proximity—undoubtedly would have converged, first culturally and eventually geopolitically.

On August 2, 1831, Joseph Smith, Sidney Rigdon, and others from Kirtland, Ohio, and members of the Colesville Branch, met at the Joshua Lewis property in Kaw Township, where they ceremonially laid a log for a school and meetinghouse and dedicated the land. "I now pronounce this land consecrated and dedicated to the Lord," said Sidney Rigdon, "for a possession and inheritance for the Saints."³¹ The following day they dedicated the temple lot on land later purchased by Bishop Partridge the following December. Before returning to Kirtland, Joseph Smith appointed those who would remain in Missouri to administer the affairs of Zion. Edward Partridge would preside as bishop. Algernon Sidney Gilbert would establish a store—the Gilbert, Whitney, and Company—named for himself and his Kirtland business partner, Newel K. Whitney. The store, which also served as the bishops' storehouse, was located in a brick wing of Gilbert's log house, and later in a brick building facing the courthouse. William W. Phelps, assisted by Oliver Cowdery and John Whitmer, would publish a newspaper, *The Evening and the Morning Star*, and the Book of Commandments, a collection of the Prophet's revelations.

Over the next two years, Bishop Partridge purchased land for the arriving Saints, as stewards over their own inheritances, and established five Mormon settlements, organizing them ecclesiastically.³² Along the western border in Kaw Township was the Prairie branch, where Lyman Wight presided.³³ Two miles east on the edge of the prairie was the

Edward Partridge was called as the first bishop of the Church and was sent to Missouri to oversee the inheritances and stewardships of the Saints gathering there.

Sidney Rigdon was designated by revelation (see D&C 58:57) to be the man to "consecrate and dedicate" the land of Zion in Missouri. He later served as a first counselor to Joseph Smith in the First Presidency from 1833 to 1844.

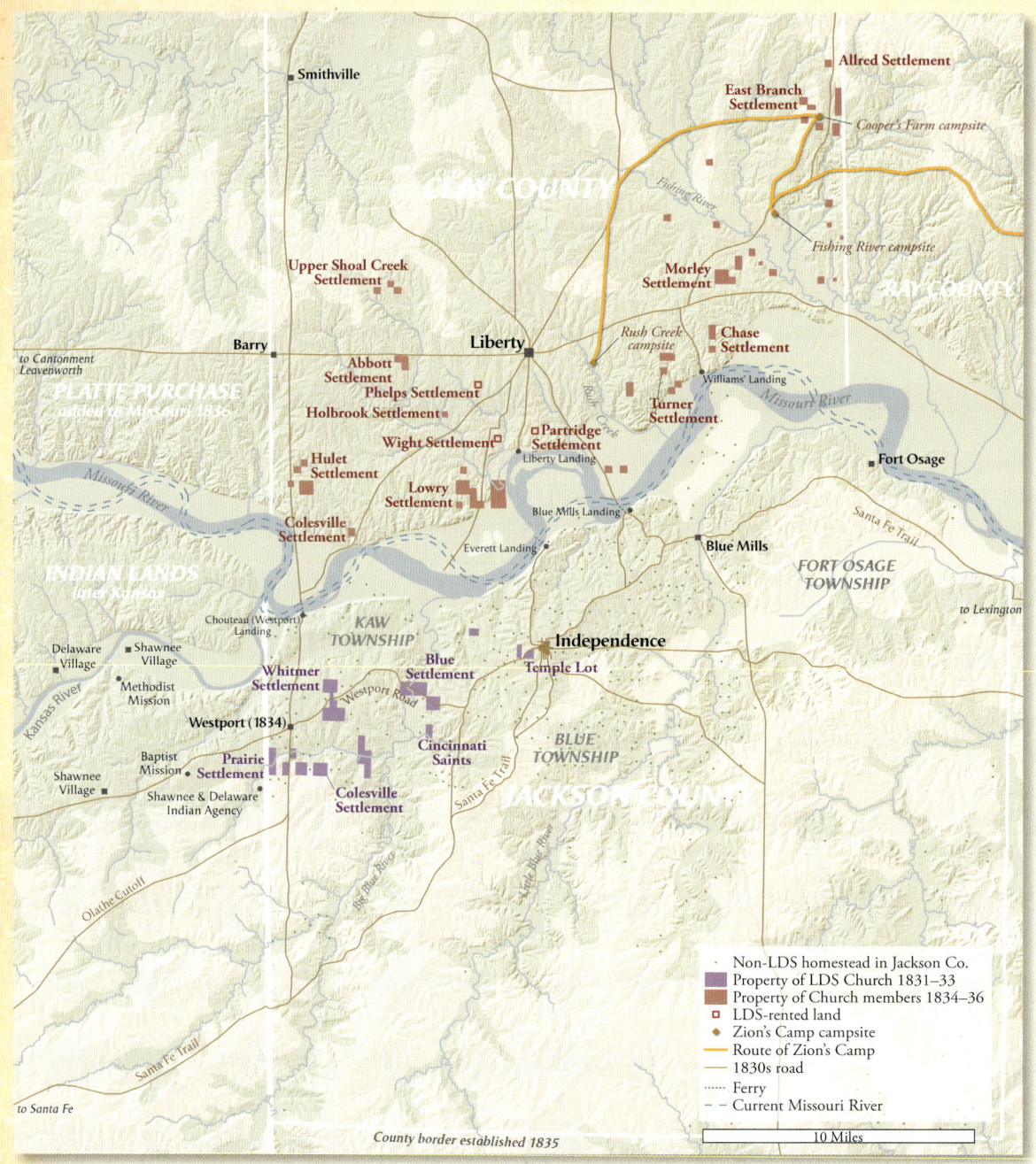

The rapid and unrestrained influx of Latter-day Saints into Jackson County from 1831 to 1833 not only gave rise to numerous settlements in the area but also caused difficulties for Bishop Edward Partridge, who was charged with the task of providing inheritances for them. The floodtide of Mormon emigrants also angered the local settlers.

Colesville settlement, where Joseph Knight Jr. and his brother Newel operated a horse-powered grist mill, and Newel served as presiding elder. Two miles north and closer to the Missouri River in heavy timber on the main Santa Fe road commenced the Whitmer settlement. Joshua Lewis lived on the south end near the newly constructed log school house, while most of the extended Whitmer family, composed of several family households, lived a mile north, with David Whitmer as the leading elder. Three miles east on the main road from Independence at the crossing of the Big Blue River, which separated Kaw from Blue Township, was the Blue River settlement, the largest of the Mormon settlements, presided over by Thomas B. Marsh. Here, Orin

Rockwell and his son Orrin Porter operated a licensed ferry. Six miles northeast of the river crossing was the temple lot on which Bishop Partridge and his counselors, Isaac Morley and John Corrill, lived; while W. W. Phelps, A. Sidney Gilbert, Oliver Cowdery, and others lived nearby in town.[34]

The doctrine of gathering was a cardinal principle of the early Mormon faithful and was intended not only for the Saints to gather to build a temple, but also to prepare for the Lord's Second Coming and to be saved from the world's impending perils. Joseph Smith's revelations and Phelps's editorials in the *Star* were the vigorous instruments of gathering. "Go ye out from Babylon," and "flee unto Zion for safety," proclaimed two revelations given in 1831.[35] The first issue of *The Evening and the Morning Star* quickly circulated this message to the eastern branches and encouraged the members to gather to Zion before the "end of the world cometh."[36] By 1833, Phelps had often reminded his readers of these warnings; and to urge others to come he would write that many had already gathered to Zion "to meet the Lord when he comes."[37] This appeal was powerful! Four hundred had arrived in western Jackson County by July 1832, and 1,200 by the following July.[38] "The church got crazy to go up to Zion," exclaimed John Corrill.[39] The disgruntled citizens cringed as each season "pours forth its swarms among us," said Robert Johnson, a citizen, who watched the Saints sometimes import their poorest members.[40] The numbers were greater than Bishop Partridge could accommodate, and he had to reduce the stewardship inheritance to ten acres or to nothing; and sometimes it was on the most "undesirable land," said John McCoy, who lived near the Mormons in Kaw Township.[41] Consequently, as the Saints continued arriving, said Corrill, "the people arose in their fury."[42]

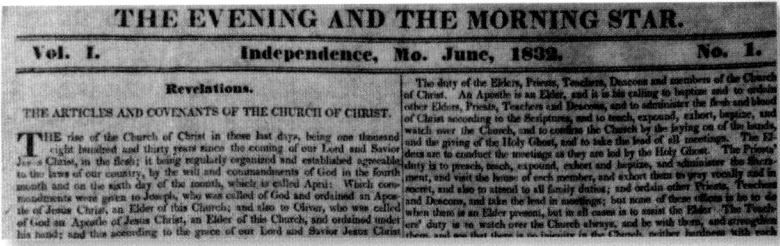

The Evening and the Morning Star was a Church-owned newspaper published monthly from Jackson County, Missouri. William W. Phelps served as editor. Through this paper, revelations, doctrine, and instruction were disseminated.

The members of the Church, however, were told not to gather unprepared and to remain in their eastern branches until they had adequate means to consecrate to the bishop in Missouri. "Be wise" and do not "build air-castles" of false expectations, Phelps cautioned. Moreover, those who arrived should have done so only after receiving a "recommend" from three elders in their eastern branch or the bishop at Kirtland, which many failed to do. "Do not let your flight BE IN HASTE, BUT LET ALL THINGS BE PREPARED BEFORE YOU," the editor of the *Star* in July 1833 boldly cautioned. However, by this late date there were already insufficient means to "plant the poor in their inheritances," warned Phelps.[43] Some of the poor, both men and women, acquired domestic and farm labor from the citizens, work that was otherwise usually done only by slaves. A few also acquired work from the McCoys, who continued to survey the Indian lands.[44]

This rush of immigration and other administrative issues caused conflict with the leaders in Ohio. Misunderstandings and administrative power struggles brought matters to a point of near crisis. A revelation in November 1832 advised the leaders in Missouri that God would "send one mighty and strong" to lead them or to replace anyone who "putteth forth his hand to steady the ark of God."[45] Oliver Cowdery said the Prophet told him that this revelation was given only as a general "caution to those in high standing," but some took offence, and problems continued.[46] By January 1833, saddened over conditions in the Church in Missouri, Orson Hyde and Hyrum Smith, representing Joseph Smith and a council of high priests at Kirtland, wrote, "We feel more like weeping over Zion than we do like rejoicing." Their letter continued, "If the people of Zion did not repent, the Lord would seek another place, and another people."[47]

Meanwhile, in order to help resolve difficulties between the two centers and to better coordinate Church business, in April 1832, Joseph Smith and his newly appointed counselors, Sidney Rigdon and Jesse Gause, along with Bishop Newel K. Whitney, traveled to Missouri to "sit in council" with the brethren in Zion. They met both to resolve past conflicts and to establish a new business enterprise, or "everlasting establishment and firm unto my church." The new firm was intended to better manage "the literary and the Mercantile establishments of my Church" and other properties and to better provide for the Church's poor, stated a revelation.[48] On April 26 at Independence, after some of the differences of the past had been "settled and the hearts of all run together in love," the brethren there were "joined together" as partners in the Church's new management company, named the United Firm. This new organization, with Joseph Smith as its leader, was designed to regulate all Church financial interests, Ohio and Missouri lands, and the bishops' storehouses, while applying principles of consecration and stewardship to the firm and its officers. Its leaders were to manage their own stewardships in the firm and be supported by it, as well as help the Church pay off its increasing debts.[49]

After Joseph Smith organized the United Firm at Independence and returned to Kirtland, his attention turned to developing plans for building the New Jerusalem. In June 1833, the leaders at Kirtland sent Partridge, Cowdery, and others at Independence a set of building instructions and drawings, including a plat map for their proposed new city and sketches for twenty-four temples—houses of the Lord or community buildings—to be constructed on the sixty-three-acre temple lot. In August, leaders sent another set of drawings and instructions

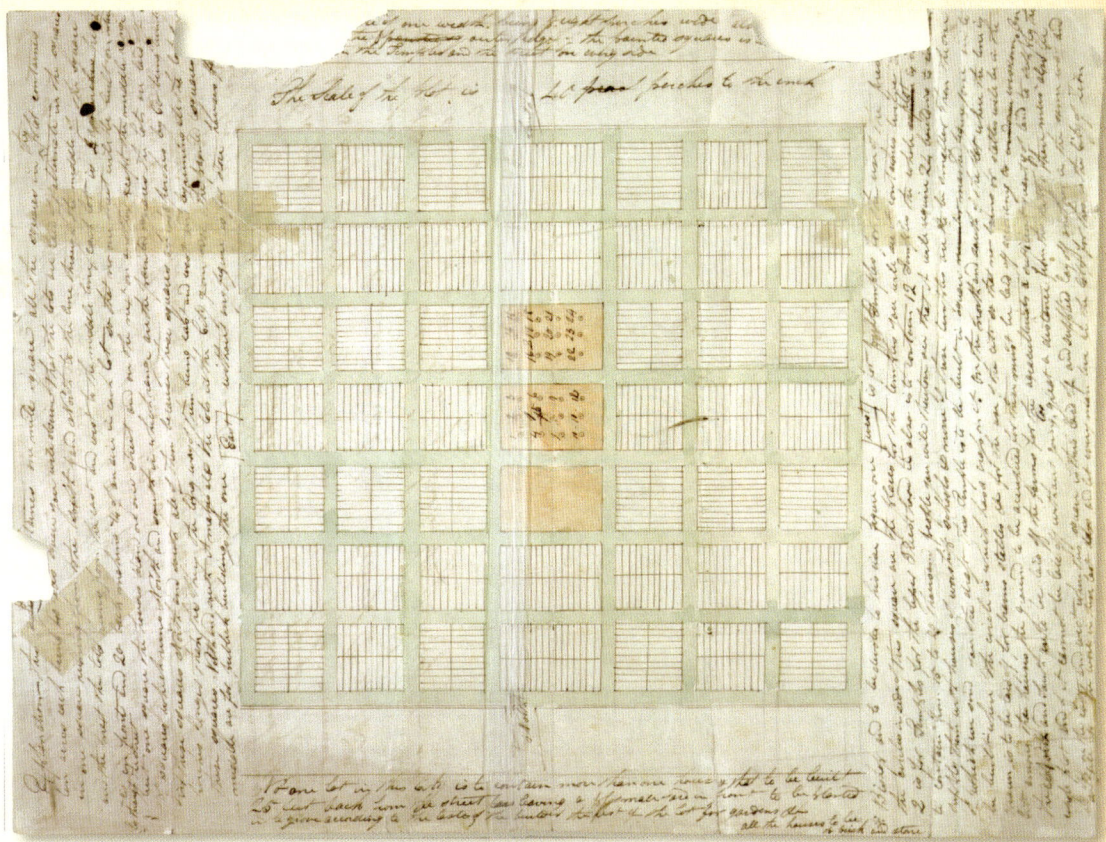

that amended the first, and enlarged both the size of the proposed city and the size of the temples.[50] The package also included instructions specifying the sequence of constructing the first three buildings. Regarding the twenty-four buildings, the schedule directed leaders first to construct three houses of the Lord, following the same plan Joseph Smith had designed for Kirtland.[51] They were to "speedily" build the first temple to be a school house, including a chapel for worship and learning (with architectural design and an interior similar to the Kirtland Temple), then near it build an office building for the Church's First Presidency, and next a printing house. These latter two structures were to follow the first as soon "as means can be obtained," the Prophet wrote.[52] Ground was never broken for any of them, however, because of lack of funds and rising hostility.

Objections to the Mormons by the local citizens soon increased in intensity and in variety. While some complained of the nuisance of the gathering and the sometimes accompanying poverty, others complained of the outward manifestations of spiritual gifts and expressed other concerns. Reverend Benton Pixley wrote that the Mormons "pretend to the gift of miracles, of tongues, of healing their sick, visions."[53] They were "visionary enthusiasts," said John C. McCoy, who spoke of "their exclusiveness, and assumption of holiness."[54] Alexander Majors, whose father later rode with the mobs, said the Mormons were "good citizens,"

In August 1833, a second plat map for the City of Zion was sent from Kirtland. This plat enlarged the city and its temples. As grand as were the plans laid out, none of these structures was ever built.

Second Plat of Zion, courtesy of the Church History Library.

Contrary to counsel, the Saints moved into Jackson County faster than land and means could be provided for them. Their zeal and indiscreet conversation about this, their new land of promise, offended many of the local citizens, causing severe reprisals.

Opposite Top: Tempers simmered among the local settlers until finally, in July 1833, violence erupted against the Latter-day Saints in Jackson County. One of the mob's first targets was the printing press where the Book of Commandments was in the process of being printed. The press was destroyed, the Book of Commandments sheets were scattered, and the building was razed.

but they sometimes in their meetings spoke in tongues, then waited for another to rise and give an interpretation.[55] The Mormons believed that these were sincere expressions of principles known on the day of Pentecost. Accordingly, by the summer of 1833, Phelps said, "Everyone that is a Saint or nearly so . . . speaks in tongues."[56]

Some complained of the Mormons being over-zealous in their claim for the land. John McCoy reported that Abel Prior, whom he considered to be a "garrulous old fanatic," and other Mormons like him, spoke "hundreds of times" of the land being theirs. "Your tract," Prior said to Isaac McCoy, "is included in my inheritance and in the Lord's own good time I will possess it."[57] David Whitmer said that some of his branch members were "continually making boasts to the Jackson county people" that excited "bitter jealousy."[58] Still other citizens complained about the future political control of the Mormons. "It requires no gift of prophesy to tell that the day is not far distant when the civil government of the county will be in their hands," wrote Robert Johnson, a citizen leader.[59] When a problem arose over local slavery in July 1833 and a concern grew that the Mormons were encouraging immigration of free people of color, Phelps instructed his people to "Shun every appearance of evil."[60] Nonetheless, Isaac McCoy said, Mormons were "filling this new county with a people among whom others could not live."[61] The younger McCoy added that this condition "gradually created a feeling of bitter hostility against them."[62] Finally, by summer 1833, the discontent of the old citizens grew furious.

OUTBREAK OF HOSTILITIES IN JACKSON COUNTY

After several minor disturbances against the Saints, such as "brick-batting" houses and burning haystacks, a committee of town and county leaders met July 18, 1833, and wrote a manifesto designed to remove the Mormons from the county—"peaceably if we can," it declared, "forcibly if we must." Two days later, on July 20, a crowd of "four or five hundred" men met at the courthouse square and ordered the Mormons to leave the county. To show its determination to remove them, the mob demonstrated violently against the Saints, damaging the Phelps printing house and family apartment and scattering the papers of the Book of Commandments into the streets. The mob threatened destruction of the Gilbert store, and tarred and feathered Bishop Edward

Partridge and Charles Allen at the north front of the courthouse to further emphasize their contempt. Three days later the mob convened again and forcibly imposed an agreement on the Mormon leaders. Half of them were to leave by the following January and the rest of the Saints by the next April, with assurance that peace would exist until they left the county.[63]

The Mormons petitioned Missouri Governor Daniel Dunklin, who advised the Mormons to seek redress through the courts. Expecting that the law would bring them justice, the Mormons hired several Liberty attorneys to assist them. However, after the citizens learned that the Mormons intended to challenge their forced agreement in the courts, the mobs began to attack the Mormon settlements. Late on the evening of October 31, a mob rode into the Whitmer settlement, whipped the men, terrorized the women and children, and ripped the roofs off of ten houses. At David Whitmer's home a mob member dragged Julia Whitmer by her hair from her house and then destroyed her home. Lydia Whiting said that as the women and children were fleeing into the woods to escape the mob, they were "frightened nearly out of their senses."[64] Philo Dibble, who lived a mile away near the Lewises, later said that as the men were being whipped, "I heard the blows of heavy ox goads upon the backs of my brethren distinctly."[65]

It was on July 20, 1833, that a mob dragged Bishop Edward Partridge and Charles Allen into the public square of Independence and ordered them to denounce their religion or leave the county. When they refused to do either, they were tarred and feathered by the mob.

The same village was attacked again on November 4. In preparation, the mob met two miles west of the Big Blue River at the store of Moses Wilson, "a restless partizan," said John C. McCoy, where Wilson regularly "formed plans, and organized raids upon the Mormon settlements."[66] From the store the mob raced west on the main road toward the Whitmer settlement. Near the Whitmer family neighborhood, the mob, bearing guns and pitchforks, confronted an arriving Mormon group from the west and a clash followed. Known as "the Battle above the Blue,"

Destroying the Press at Independence by John Thompson; courtesy of the Church History Library. Tarring and Feathering of Bishop Partridge © Glen S. Hopkinson; for more information, visit www.glenhopkinson.com.

the skirmish left two of the mob and a Mormon dead, and several on both sides wounded, including Wilson's son.[67]

Meanwhile, on November 1, at Independence, a mob damaged Mormon houses, shops, and A. Sidney Gilbert's brick store. The following day a mob attacked the Blue River branch, taking over the ferry, destroying houses, and beating David Bennett. Then on November 5, just west of the temple lot, a confrontation occurred between the Mormons and the state militia under the command of Colonel Thomas Pitcher. The militia, on the pretext of maintaining order, confiscated the guns of the Mormons, as Lt. Governor Lilburn W. Boggs, a town resident, looked on.[68] Once the Mormons were defenseless, the citizens began to drive them from the county. "The settlers were the aggressors so far as overt acts were concerned," said John C. McCoy. The fact is, he continued, "the Mormons received at the hands of their Gentile neighbors very harsh treatment. . . . It was cruel."[69]

EXPULSION FROM JACKSON COUNTY

Beginning November 6, "women and children fled in every direction, before a merciless mob," wrote Parley P. Pratt. Some fled southward to Van Buren County, others east to Lafayette and Ray counties, but most crossed the Missouri River into Clay County at points along a fifteen-mile sweep of the river.[70] On November 7, crowds amassed at Independence landing, three miles north of the temple lot. Emily Partridge said of the hundreds present: "Some in tents, and some in the open air, around their fires, while the rain descended in torrents." She continued, "Husbands were enquiring for their wives, and women for their husbands, parents for children, and children for parents," some with provisions, some without. "The scene was indescribable."[71] It took two weeks at Independence landing using Everett's ferry to get the Saints at that site across the river. After the exiles were driven from their homes, their "fields of corn were plundered and destroyed," Pratt noted. Stacks of wheat were burned, and Pratt's own household goods were either destroyed or stolen.[72]

After the Saints crossed the Missouri River, conditions in Clay County remained poignant.

The treatment that the Mormons received at the hands of Jackson County citizens was cruel. Emily Partridge Young recounted the torrential rains that fell on the refugees while they huddled in the open air around their fires. The scene, she said, "was indescribable."

Emily Partridge, courtesy of the Church Archives, The Church of Jesus Christ of Latter-day Saints.

Scattered for miles along the river bottoms in groups, the expatriates "exposed their wives and little ones to the cold and chilling blasts of winter without shelter," wrote Joseph Thorpe, a Clay County farmer and later judge.[73] Late in December, while in a near state of starvation and while camped by a huge sycamore log used for a wall and with a blanket for a cover, Harriet Wight gave birth to a son, Lyman Lehi Wight.[74] Emily Austin, a member of the Colesville branch, still clinging to her neighbors at the river bottoms, said: "We lived in tents until winter set in, and did our cooking out in the wind and storms. Log heaps were our parlor stoves, and the cold, wet ground our velvet carpets. And the crying of little children our piano forte."[75] From the north bank of the Missouri River in December, Phelps wrote to Joseph Smith for help: "The situation of the saints, as scattered . . . affords a gloomy prospect," he said. "Our cloths are worn out—we want the necessaries of life."[76]

In their search for the Promised Land, the distressed little multitude had not lived up to its ideals—some had disobeyed counsel, while others had used poor judgment. In his same December 1833 letter to Joseph Smith, Phelps wrote: "I know it was right that we should be driven out of the land of Zion, that the rebellious might be sent away."[77] At Kirtland a month later, a revelation said of the exiled Saints, "They have been afflicted, in consequence of their transgressions."[78] In its sacred quest for the Holy City, Zion stumbled.

The exiled Saints survived the winter and spring by working for the friendly local citizens of Clay County. Michael Arthur, a slave owner, industrialist, and farmer, employed several destitute Mormons. John Whitmer soon rented a house from Arthur, worked at his whisky still, borrowed money from him, and pulled corn for a neighbor, Shabael Allen.[79] Parley P. Pratt wrote that he was "reduced to the lowest poverty." He continued, "I made a living by day labor, jobbing, building, or wood cutting."[80] Lyman Wight worked at Arthur's mill and helped build a house for him. When spring work was available, Joseph Thorpe said, "The Mormons, in the main, were industrious, good workers, and

The driving of the Saints from Jackson County was a devastating blow to the entire Church, members of which had placed so much hope in this new land of Zion. In this letter from the Prophet Joseph Smith, dated December 10, 1833, he confessed "there are two things of which I am ignorant. . . . Why God hath suffered so great calamity to come upon Zion . . . and again by what means he will return her to her inheritance."

gave general satisfaction to their employers, and could live on less than any people I ever knew."[81]

After the Mormons were driven from Jackson County, they quickly sought criminal prosecution in the courts for the crimes they had suffered. Governor Daniel Dunklin authorized a court of inquiry and sent Robert W. Wells, the state's attorney general, to Independence to observe the hearings during the February 1834 term of the circuit court. Nevertheless, even with the state militia present, which had guarded the Mormon witnesses from Clay County, the severity of the mob spirit and citizen intimidation against the witnesses were so out of control that both Wells and the circuit attorney recommended an end to the hearings. Eventually, the suits and legal process progressed so slowly and were so costly to the Mormons that they dropped them.[82] A revelation to Joseph Smith directed Missouri Church leaders to seek redress through the local courts, and to petition Missouri officials (specifically Governor Dunklin), and even U.S. President Andrew Jackson (who passed the request to Secretary of War, Lewis Cass). Ultimately, however, all failed.[83]

Attempts for civil redress at Independence also failed to obtain judgments. As special test cases, however, Phelps and Partridge received a change of venue to have their cases tried in Richmond, Ray County.[84] In 1836 the circuit court there finally made a decision in their favor. Although Phelps had asked for $50,000 for the destruction of his brick-press building, including his residence, the press, its equipment and book supplies, the court rendered him "the sum of seven hundred and fifty dollars." For the assault upon Edward Partridge by the accused, Robert Johnson and others, for beating him with "many violent blows" and tarring and feathering him at the square in Independence in July 1833, the court awarded Bishop Partridge a disheartening judgment of "one cent."[85]

ZION'S CAMP

Governor Daniel Dunklin offered to use the state militia to escort the Mormons back to Jackson County once they petitioned a request. However, if they returned to their lands, the Mormons would have to protect themselves from further violence in Jackson County, which gave need for the presence of a protective local Mormon force.[86] Upon receiving a revelation on February 24, 1834, to organize a quasi-military-police and relief party to aid the exiled Mormons

William Wines Phelps was among those who filed suit for the loss of his Jackson County property. He asked for $50,000 and was awarded $750. Edward Partridge similarly filed and was awarded one cent in damages.

Opposite Bottom: Some two hundred men enlisted in Zion's Camp. The men marched about eight hundred miles from Ohio to Missouri for the purpose of joining forces with the Missouri State Militia and reestablishing the Saints on their Jackson County lands.

in Clay County, Joseph Smith was elected by the Kirtland high council "Commander in Chief of the Armies of Israel," later known as Zion's Camp, to lead this operation.[87] Eventually, some 205 men enlisted.

During the first week of May 1834, the first group of Mormon defenders left Ohio and Michigan headed for Missouri. Unfortunately, just before the departure of the Ohio contingent, the postmaster in nearby Chagrin, Ohio, sent a letter to the postmaster in Independence stating with exaggerated numbers that from two to six hundred Mormons had organized to "take by force of arms their possessions in Jackson County."[88] When the news reached Missouri's western counties, an immediate alarm was sounded among the local citizens to prepare for what they considered a belligerent invasion. In June, after a six-week, eight-hundred-mile journey, Zion's Camp arrived in eastern Clay County. It was at this time that an unnamed Lexington, Lafayette County, resident wrote to his father in Mason County, Kentucky, "the whole country is in an uproar" and there will be "much blood shed."[89] However, on June 19, a large and violent summer storm struck at the mob's campsite, preventing the frenzied citizens from attacking.[90]

On June 21, while camped near Fishing River in Clay County, Joseph Smith and the leaders of Zion's Camp met with Clay County Sheriff Cornelius Gilliam and Colonel John Sconce of Ray County to clarify their objective and to correct false rumors about their mission.

Missouri Governor Daniel Dunklin offered to call up the state's militia to assist in escorting the Mormons back into Jackson County to reclaim their property. This offer, coupled with a revelation from the Lord (see D&C 103), led to the formation of Zion's Camp.

When Zion's Camp reached Missouri, enraged citizens swore that the Mormons would "see hell before morning." As the mobs gathered to attack, a storm arose of such fury that it flooded rivers, downed trees, and scattered the mobs. The timely intervention saved the outnumbered soldiers of Zion's Camp.

Following the discussion, the leaders on both sides signed a document of accord: "It is not our intention to commence hostilities against any man, . . . person or property."[91] Fortunately for the Mormons, the peace agreement pacified the locals, several hundred of whom had gathered from neighboring counties to fight the Mormons. Had peace not been negotiated, "no quarter would have been given," wrote one county regulator. "We could have killed most of them before they got across the river."[92] On June 22, the day after signing the truce, a revelation to the Prophet informed the Saints that they would have to "wait for a little season, for the redemption of Zion."[93]

On July 23, Zion's Camp marched toward Liberty, camping in the field of George Burkett, one of the exiled Mormons, near Rush Creek, two miles east of the Clay County courthouse. Here, members of Zion's Camp were stricken with a deadly attack of cholera, leaving fifteen dead, including two Mormons who lived nearby: Algernon Sidney Gilbert and six-year-old Phebe Murdock.[94]

Joseph Smith next moved to Lyman Wight's residence—an old log cabin at Michael Arthur's farm, four miles south of Liberty—and on July 3 assisted Wight in discharging members of Zion's Camp. On July 7, while at the Arthur property, the Prophet organized the Missouri presidency, with David Whitmer designated as president of the Church in Zion, William W. Phelps and John Whitmer as counselors, and a high council of twelve men to assist.[95] With the Missouri leadership organized, Joseph Smith and most of the camp members returned to Kirtland.

Zion's Camp by Judith Mehr; courtesy of the Church Archives, The Church of Jesus Christ of Latter-day Saints.

Four key messages in the revelation received at Fishing River directed the activities of the Saints in Missouri for the next two years: (1) Zion was to be redeemed after a designated "little season"; (2) the Saints were to remain in Clay County; (3) the Church would continue to gather to Clay County to make ready for another attempt to redeem Zion; and (4) certain Missouri Church leaders were to receive a spiritual "endowment" in the temple at Kirtland.[96] Concerning the anticipated return to Zion, after returning to Ohio, Joseph Smith, on August 16, 1834, wrote to the leaders in Clay County, giving the date for the return: "Two years from the Eleventh of September next [September 11, 1836] . . . is the appointed time for the redemption of Zion."[97] Hence, they had two years to prepare to return to Jackson County.

To promote the second message, that of gathering, the leaders in Missouri were told to take the initiative and encourage members living in the East to gather to Clay County and be ready to move in force into Jackson County at the appointed time. As the Saints gathered, they were told to do so diplomatically and to be mindful of the Clay County citizens. "And let all my people who dwell in the regions round about be very faithful, and prayerful, and humble before me, and reveal not the things which I have revealed unto them," the revelation counseled, and "talk not of judgments, neither boast of faith nor of mighty works."[98] As additional Mormon emigrants began arriving in Clay County in 1835, and in greater numbers in 1836, some purchased land, as did the exiled members, until they owned more than 3,600 acres in the county. These lands, privately owned, were not administered under the Church's consecration rules. In settling Clay County, the Latter-day Saints established fourteen settlements or Mormon neighborhoods along a twenty-five-mile stretch at the southern end and lower eastern edge of the county, with an increasing population of more than a thousand members of the Church.[99]

On June 23, 1834, members of Zion's Camp —among them Joseph and Hyrum Smith—were attacked with the dread disease of cholera. Before its course was stayed, sixty-eight of their number had contracted the disease and thirteen members of the camp had died.

The revelation given at Fishing River also instructed the Church to gather "my warriors" to Clay County. Before returning to Kirtland in 1834, Joseph Smith began to make plans for a second

Zion's Camp, with David Whitmer as its leader. A year later, on September 24, 1835, Joseph Smith and the Kirtland High Council "appointed David Whitmer Capt. of the Lord's host" and Frederick G. Williams and Sidney Rigdon his assistants, reported John Whitmer.[100] In his own journal on that September date, Joseph Smith recorded: "This day drew up an Article of enrollment for the redemption of Zion that we may obtain volunteers to go next Spring to Missouri." Continuing, he said, "I ask God in the name of Jesus that we may obtain Eight hundred men (or one thousand) well armed." The Prophet was resolute: "We go next season to live or die in Jackson County."[101] In March 1836, Joseph set the departure of their "removing to Zion" to be "on or before the 15th of May." Thus, it would be shortly after the Kirtland Temple dedication and four months before the September deadline.[102]

Before Joseph Smith ever left Missouri in 1834, plans were made for a second Zion's Camp to return the Saints to their land. On September 24, 1835, David Whitmer was titled "Captain of the Lord's Host" and was appointed to lead that army back into Jackson County. However, later deliberations in council abandoned that plan, and a second Zion's Camp was never organized.

THE KIRTLAND ENDOWMENT

Meanwhile, leaders in Clay County had been called to Kirtland to help build the temple, to generally aid the Church, and to help prepare for a strong return to Jackson County. In 1835, W. W. Phelps and John Whitmer were assigned to assist with the publication of *The Latter-day Saints' Messenger and Advocate*, and Phelps was to publish the Doctrine and Covenants, containing the revelations of Joseph Smith. Since this publication would include revelations about the United Firm organized at Independence, Church leaders desired to protect from unwarranted litigation their business interests as described in five revelations about the firm to be included in the new book of scripture. The United Firm had been dissolved after two troubled years of heavy debt, partly because of unexpected losses suffered at Independence in 1833. Consequently, leaders decided to publish the revelations about the firm by using protective fictitious words or code names in place of certain nouns used in the revelations, including disguising the firm's name.[103] Moreover, in addition to the presence of the above two leaders, Bishop Partridge, David Whitmer, John Corrill, and others from Missouri were at Kirtland to receive their spiritual enrichment or "endowment" in connection with the events associated with the temple dedication, as they had been promised in the June 1834 revelation.[104]

On March 29, two days after the temple dedication, Joseph Smith, Frederick G. Williams, Sidney Rigdon, Hyrum Smith, and Oliver Cowdery met together to receive their final instructions before

David Whitmer, courtesy of the Church History Library.

they journeyed west to redeem Zion. Since all preparations had been completed or were about to be, the above presidency of the Church "sought for a revelation from [God] to teach us concerning our going to Zion," wrote Joseph Smith.[105] However, on April 2, Church leaders, including "Captain" David Whitmer, met again and, "after mature deliberation," dropped their plans to redeem Zion; the second Zion's Camp effort was not spoken of again. Instead, the leaders authorized money to buy other land in Missouri.[106]

MORMON RESETTLEMENT IN CALDWELL COUNTY AND DAVIESS COUNTY

After the temple was dedicated, four "wise men"—Bishop Edward Partridge, William W. Phelps, Isaac Morley, and John Corrill—returned to Missouri with money to buy land in the unorganized territory attached to Ray County. Upon their return they searched out possible locations where the main body of the Church "could settle in peace," John Whitmer wrote.[107] This shift in plans was timely. Once again, agitation against the Latter-day Saints in Clay County had already begun. The old residents had never considered allowing the Mormons to remain in the county permanently. Yet the fact that many citizens feared the growing Mormon presence and the possibility of them gaining political dominance, similar to those expressed earlier in Jackson County, induced rage among the citizens. "The poor, deluded mortals, with all their experience in Jackson began to tell the citizens of Clay the same old tale," wrote Joseph Thorpe, "that this country was theirs by gift of the Lord." He continued, "This kind of talk, with their insolence and imprudent behavior so enraged the citizens that they began to consult about the best course to take to rid themselves of a set of religious fanatics," as they viewed them.[108]

To remedy the situation, community leaders, including some friends of the Mormons, held a meeting at the Liberty courthouse on June 29, 1836, to discuss some options. Though without the "least right, under the constitution," they persuaded the Mormons to leave the county. The temper at the meeting was volatile, and the committee advised the Mormons to avoid a future bloody conflict by seeking "a home where they may obtain large and separate bodies of land and have a community of their own."[109] On July 1, the Mormon leaders agreed that the Saints, as asked, would stop immigration and find a new place to settle "for the sake of friendship and to be in a covenant of peace," wrote W. W. Phelps.[110]

Unfortunately, violence against the Saints had already begun with fervor in the eastern part of Clay County. Vigilantes stopped Mormon wagons coming from the East on the main road and turned them back

Though the Latter-day Saints had been initially welcomed as refugees into Clay County, that welcome soon wore thin, and some of the old settlers in Clay County turned to violent and other unlawful measures to remove the Mormons from the county. Few things could invoke as much terror among the Saints as an angry mob.

to neighboring Ray County. "They have been flocking in here faster than ever and making great talk what they would do," said Anderson Wilson, a mob leader.[111] Drusilla Hendricks and her husband, James, having recently arrived, found that the old citizens were afraid that the "Mormons would . . . take away their place and nation," wrote Drusilla.[112] The citizens acknowledged that they were violating the peace and "trampling" on the "law and Constitution, but we cannot help it," Wilson declared. Indeed, several outrages were committed against the Mormons. During one incident a mob "took a mormon out of company & gave him 100 lashes and it is thought he will die of this beating." Referring to his volunteer companies of raiders patrolling the roads of eastern Clay County, Wilson said that they would "fight by each other's side and die" if necessary in driving the Mormons from the county.[113] But the Mormons quickly agreed with Phelps's pledge and soon began to move.

In preparation, William W. Phelps and Edward Partridge had by July 7 filed for twenty parcels of eighty acres of land in a largely uninhabited region. "We found a mill seat on Shoal Creek, about 35 miles N. E. of Liberty," Partridge wrote, "that suited us very well, north of Ray County, in an unorganized territory."[114] To further clear their way, John Corrill and John Murdock met with Ray County officials to receive permission to settle in the area, which at that time was attached to Ray County. The Ray County committee, however, demanded that all Mormons who had been turned out of Clay County, and those still on the road, leave their county immediately, as well as the refugees from Jackson County who had settled earlier on Crooked River. They also set a buffer zone of approximately six miles north of what was then the northern boundary line of Ray County, where Mormons were not to settle.[115] W. W. Phelps, John Whitmer, and Edward Partridge soon began to organize the town of Far West, the new Mormon center, in what would soon be Caldwell County. In late December 1836, the Missouri legislature created Caldwell County (for the Mormons) and Daviess County to the north, which legislation was signed into law by the newly elected governor, Lilburn W. Boggs.[116]

In 1837, while the Latter-day Saints in Missouri enjoyed relative peace and prosperity in their new locale, Kirtland was crumbling because of leadership dissension and financial and legal problems. Facing vexatious litigation and physical threats against his life, Joseph Smith, on January 12, 1838, fled Kirtland for Missouri, where he arrived at Far West two months later on March 14. However, by this time, problems had emerged among the Missouri leadership. Four days before the Prophet's arrival, the Missouri high council at Far West had excommunicated two members of the Missouri presidency—William W. Phelps and John Whitmer—for misconduct. One month later, on April 12, the high council excommunicated Oliver Cowdery, and a day later David Whitmer, both over matters of personal faithfulness.[117]

In spite of the disaffections, Church leaders remained optimistic regarding the future prospects of the Church in northern Missouri and planned for additional settlements. On May 18, Joseph Smith traveled north to Daviess County to select a site for a settlement on the Grand River at Spring Hill, which they subsequently named Adam-ondi-Ahman. During a visit there a month later, the Prophet appointed his uncle, John Smith, stake president, with Reynolds Cahoon and Lyman Wight as counselors.

In 1836, the Missouri legislature created two new counties in northern Missouri—Caldwell and Daviess counties. Caldwell County was created especially for the Mormons.

During spring and early summer the Prophet received several significant revelations that enriched the Church. On April 26, a revelation clarified the official name of the Church to be "The Church of Jesus Christ of Latter Day Saints."[118] The following month a revelation designated Adam-ondi-Ahman in Daviess County as the "place where Adam shall come to visit his people."[119] And on July 8, Joseph Smith presented the Church with a new financial system, the law of tithing. Consecration as earlier taught and practiced was now modified; Church members were to "pay one-tenth of all their income annually." Thereafter, this became the standard financial rule.[120] That same July day a revelation appointed four new Apostles

MAP BY JOHN HAMER

Map by John Hamer.

It was May 18, 1838, when the Prophet Joseph Smith traveled north into Daviess County. He visited the home of Lyman Wight, who lived in a small cabin overlooking the Grand River. It was near there that Joseph directed the laying out of the city of Adam-ondi-Ahman.

to replace those who had fallen amid the Kirtland problems, namely John Taylor, John E. Page, Wilford Woodruff, and Willard Richards.[121]

By 1838, the Mormons living in northern Missouri were strengthened by the presence of Joseph Smith, in addition to hundreds of Latter-day Saints who had moved to the region from Ohio. The new name of the Church clarified its Christian identity. The implementation of tithing increased the prospect of financial security and stability. And the appointment of four new Apostles energized the Church's leadership. A new spiritual optimism prevailed. The future of the new Zion looked promising and full of hope. However, dark clouds of persecution were on the horizon, and a war—The Mormon War—would result.

NOTES

1. Journal History of The Church of Jesus Christ of Latter-day Saints, January 13, 1831, 1; January 29, 1831, 2; Church History Library, Salt Lake City, Utah (hereafter referred to as CHL). The Journal History gives Peterson's full name as Richard Ziba Peterson.

2. Robin Scott Jensen, Robert J. Woodford, and Steven C. Harper, eds., *Revelations and Translations, Volume 1: Manuscript Revelation Books*, vol. 1 of the Revelations and Translations series of *The Joseph Smith Papers*, ed. Dean C. Jessee, Ronald K. Esplin, and Richard Lyman Bushman (Salt Lake City: The Church Historian's Press, 2011), 52 [D&C 28:8–9] (hereafter cited as *JSP*, R1).

3. Journal History, October 1830, 6. Oliver Cowdery's commission was dated Manchester, New York, October 17, 1830, and signed by him with an addendum of loyalty signed by Peter Whitmer Jr., Parley P. Pratt, and Ziba Peterson. See Eber D. Howe, *Mormonism Unvailed* (Painesville, OH: 1834), 212–213.

4. Parley P. Pratt, *Autobiography of Parley Parker Pratt* (Salt Lake City, UT: Deseret Book Company, 1985), 40.

5. See Eleanor Atkinson, "The Winter of the Deep Snow," *Transactions of the Illinois State Historical Society for the Year 1909* (Springfield, IL: State Journal Co., 1910):47–62. See also "Snow–Snow. Accounts of heavy falls of snow . . . all the way to Council Bluffs," *Missouri Republican* (St. Louis), February 8, 1831, 3. In late January 1831, Oliver Cowdery wrote from Jackson County: "The weather is quite severe, and the snow is considerably deep." Journal History, January 29, 1831, 1. A copy of Cowdery's letter was also included in a letter of Joseph Smith to Hyrum Smith, March 3–4, 1831, as cited in Michael Hubbard MacKay, Gerrit J. Dirkmaat, Grant Underwood, Robert J. Woodford, and William G. Hartley, eds., *Documents, Volume 1: July 1828–June 1831*, vol. 1 of the Documents series of *The Joseph Smith Papers*, ed. Dean C. Jessee, Ronald K. Esplin, and Richard Lyman Bushman (Salt Lake City: The Church Historian's Press, 2013), 272–273 (hereafter cited as *JSP*, D1).

6. Grant Foreman, *Indian Removal* (Norman, OK: University of Oklahoma Press, 1953), 21. Jackson County was named for General Andrew Jackson, who was not elected president until 1828, but who had gained fame for earlier military successes. See *History of Jackson County, Missouri* (Kansas City, MO: Union Historical Company, 1881), 66, 101. Until 1825, Jackson County had been occupied by the Osage Indians, and the area just west of Missouri by the Kaw or Kanza Indians. In 1825, the tribes were moved away, allowing Jackson County to be organized in 1826. The seat of the county was named Independence for General Jackson's "independence of character." See W. L. Webb, *The Centennial History of Independence, Mo.* (Independence, MO: W. L. Webb, 1927), 28.

7. See C. A. Weslager, *The Delaware Indian Westward Migration: With the Texts of Two Manuscripts (1821–22) Responding to General Lewis Cass's Inquiries about Lenape Culture and Language* (Wallingford, PA: Middle Atlantic, 1978), 209–219; C. A. Westlager, *The Delaware Indians: A History* (New Brunswick, NJ: Rutgers University Press, 1972), 360–371; *Walam Olum or Red Score: The Migration Legend of the Lenni Lenape or Delaware Indians* (Indianapolis, IN: Indiana Historical Society, 1954), 215n, 251–253. See also Lela Barnes, "Journal of Isaac McCoy for the Exploring Expedition of 1830," *Kansas Historical Quarterly* 5, no. 4 (November 1936):344–345; Esther Clark Hill, "Some Background of Early Baptist Missions in Kansas," *Kansas Historical Quarterly* 1, no. 2 (February 1932):89; and Warren A. Jennings, "First Mormon Mission to the Indians," *Kansas Historical Quarterly* 37, no. 3 (Autumn 1971):292–294. Isaac McCoy's 1830 survey map shows the Delaware settlement around Mill Creek, situated a few miles west of the Missouri state line and north of the Kansas River. See Isaac McCoy papers, Kansas State Historical Society, Topeka, Kansas.

The previous summer, Isaac McCoy, a government surveyor, surveyed the Delaware reservation, including marking off land at its northern edge for the establishment of Ft. Leavenworth, a small frontier military garrison. McCoy, a licensed Baptist minister and principal agent of the government for relocating these tribes, had extensively appealed to them to establish Baptist missions and schools among them, but had failed. See Earl Leon Shoup, "Indian Missions in Kansas," *Collections of the Kansas State Historical Society, 1911–1912* (Topeka: State Printing Office, 1912); Barnes, "Journal of Isaac McCoy," 341–345, 376; Isaac McCoy, *History of the Baptist Indian Missions* (Washington, DC: William M. Morrison, 1840), 404–405; John Calvin McCoy, "Survey of Kansas Indian Lands," *Transactions of the Kansas State Historical Society*, vol. 4 (Topeka: Kansas State Printing Co., 1890):300; George A. Shultz, *An Indian Canaan* (Norman, OK: University of Oklahoma Press, 1972), 30. As early as November 30, 1818, in Indiana, Chief Anderson told McCoy that the Delawares wanted nothing to do with his religion, which view continued until the chief's death in 1831. Jennings, "First Mormon Mission to the Indians," 299.

In the fall of 1830, Thomas Johnson, a Methodist minister, received authorization to establish a Shawnee Methodist mission west of Jackson County. That season, he built a large, two-story log structure six miles west of the border and three miles south of the Kansas River, preparing to open his Indian school in the spring. See J. J. Lutz, "The Methodist Missions Among the Indian Tribes in Kansas," *Transactions of the Kansas State Historical Society*, vol. 9 (Topeka: Kansas State Printing Office, 1906):160–169; John Endacott, comp., "Addresses at the Dedication of the Monument at Turner," *Collections of the Kansas State Historical Society*, vol. 14 (Topeka: Kansas State Printing, 1918): 187–197; Barnes, "Journal of Isaac McCoy," 375–377 and n45 and n46. Likewise, in late 1830, Johnston Lykins, a Baptist minister and Isaac McCoy's son-in-law, had successfully negotiated with the Shawnees and the government to establish the first Shawnee Baptist Mission, three miles west of the Missouri border, which he did in 1831. See McCoy, *History of Baptist Indian Mission*, 413; Hill, "Some Background of Early Baptist Missions in Kansas," 90 and notes; Shoup, "Indian Missions in Kansas," 67.

8. Pratt, *Autobiography*, 41; Cowdery later wrote: "We understand there are many among the Shawnees who also believe." Oliver Cowdery to My dearly beloved brethren, April 8, 1831, Kirtland Letter Book, 11, CHL.

9. Pratt, *Autobiography*, 41. Chief Anderson would have been about seventy years old.

10. Pratt wrote that "some forty men collected." Pratt, *Autobiography*, 42. Cowdery wrote that there were eighteen or twenty men. Oliver Cowdery to the Brethren in Ohio, in Journal History, January 29, 1831, 1. See also *JSP*, D1:272.

11. Journal History, January 29, 1831, 2.

12. Oliver Cowdery to William Clark, February 14, 1831, William Clark Papers, vol. 6, 103, Kansas State Historical Society, Topeka, Kansas, hereafter cited as Clark Papers. Clark and Meriwether Lewis were the famous expedition leaders of the Lewis and Clark expedition that explored the upper Louisiana Purchase in 1804–1806.

13. Richard W. Cummins to William Clark, February 15, 1832, Clark Papers, vol. 6, 103.

14. William General Clark was away from his office in St. Louis from November 30, 1830, to March 31, 1831. See Jennings, "The First Mormon Mission to the Indians," 298. Cowdery optimistically expected Pratt to return with a government permit. Oliver Cowdery to My dearly beloved brethren & sisters in the Lord, April 8, 1831, *JSP*, D1:293.

15. Pratt, *Autobiography*, 44.

16. Journal History, January 29, 1831, 2. Using the 1830 U.S. census and early Jackson County branch lists, Ronald E. Romig identified eight families in Jackson County who became early members of the Church. See Ronald E. Romig, "The Lamanite Mission," *John Whitmer Historical Association Journal* 14 (1994): 30. John C. McCoy, a neighbor of Mormons in Kaw Township, said the Mormons had in total "very few converts among the Gentiles, perhaps not a dozen in all." John C. McCoy, "A Famous Town," *Kansas City Journal*, January 18, 1885, 8.

17. Oliver Cowdery may have resided with the Joshua Lewis family that spring, since he dates his letters from Kaw Township, the county's third and westernmost township. See Dean Jessee, "Joseph Knight's Recollection of Early Mormon History," *BYU Studies* 17, no. 1 (Autumn 1976): 39. By late 1833, the road west from Independence became known as the Westport Road, named for Westport, where John C. McCoy built a store near the state line. See John C. McCoy, "Life in the 'Far West,'" *Kansas City Journal*, November 18, 1883, n. p.

18. By 1833, Ziba Peterson became disaffected from Mormonism and remained in Lafayette County until 1848, when he emigrated to California. He settled in Dry Diggins, El Dorado County, where he was elected sheriff in January 1849, and officiated at the first legal hanging in the state of California. He died sometime before June 1849, leaving a large family. After the hanging, the community of Dry Diggins changed its name to Hangtown, and later to Placerville. Rebecca Hopper Peterson died in Napa County, California, in 1896. See H. Dean Garrett, "Ziba Peterson: From Missionary to Hanging Sheriff," *Nauvoo Journal* 9, no. 1 (Spring 1997): 28–32; and Irene Johnson, "The Other Missionary—Ziba Peterson," unpublished paper presented to Mormon History Association, 1991, CHL.

19. Oliver Cowdery to Our dearly beloved Brethren, May 7, 1831, *JSP*, D1:296–97.

20. John Mason Peck, *A New Guide for Emigrants to the West*, 2nd ed. (Boston: Gould, Kendall and Lincoln, 1837), 115, 119, 121; John Mason Peck, *Forty Years of Pioneer Life, Memoir of John Mason Peck D. D.* (Carbondale, IL: Southern Illinois University Press, reprint, 1965), 144-150, 159.

21. See John Treat Irving Jr., *Indian Sketches, Taken During an Expedition to the Pawnee Tribes*, ed. John Francis McDermott (Norman, OK: University of Oklahoma Press, 1955) xxi, 11–12.

22. Webb, *The Centennial History of Independence*, 92–93. Sometimes the fighting was violent, including the use of daggers and the gouging out of eyes. Hatti M. Anderson, "The Evolution of a Frontier Society in Missouri, 1815–1828, Part 1," *Missouri Historical Review* 32, no. 3 (April 1938):311.

23. William W. Phelps, "Extract of Letter, Independence, Jackson County, July 23, 1831," *Ontario Phoenix*, (September 7, 1831): n.p.

24. John C. McCoy, "The Other Side," *Kansas City Journal*, April 24, 1881, 9.

25. *JSP*, R1:78 [D&C 42:32–36].

26. *JSP*, R1:221–222 [D&C 70]; Donald Q. Cannon and Lyndon Cook, eds., *Far West Record, Minutes of the Church of Jesus Christ of Latter-day Saints, 1830–1844* (Salt Lake City: Deseret Book Company, 1983), 30–32.

27. Jessee, "Joseph Knight's Recollection of Early Mormon History," 39.

28. Joseph Smith, "To the Elders of the Church," *Latter Day Saints' Messenger and Advocate* 1, no. 12 (September 1835): 179.

29. *JSP*, R1:122 [D&C 57:3].

30. Ezra Booth, "To Rev. Ira Eddy," *Ohio Star*, 2, no. 46 (November 17, 1831): 3.

31. Karen Lynn Davidson, Richard L. Jensen, and David J. Whitaker, eds., *Histories 2, Assigned Histories, 1831–1847*, vol. 2 of the Histories series of *The Joseph Smith Papers*, ed. Dean C. Jessee, Ronald K. Esplin, and Richard Lyman Bushman (Salt Lake City: The Church Historians Press, 2012), 44 (hereafter cited as *JSP*, H2). The location of the unmarked site of the Church school and the dedication of Zion is at 1707 East 35th St., Kansas City, Missouri. The log school burned down on June 28, 1913. See *Kansas City Journal*, November 29, 1925, 1.

32. Edward Partridge indicated that he held title in his name to 2,136 acres of Church property in Jackson County. Clark V. Johnson, ed., *Mormon Redress Petitions: Documents of the 1833–1838 Missouri Conflict* (Provo, UT: Religious Study Center, Brigham Young University, 1992), 513. On September 11, 1833, the five settlements were reorganized

into ten ecclesiastical branches. See Cannon and Cook, *Far West Record*, 65.

33. Lyman Wight wrote: "[I] had the watch care of a branch of 160 members, in which branch I preached three times every Sabbath and once every Thursday." Lyman Wight, untitled history with a letter to Wilford Woodruff, 7, August 24, 1857, CHL. In 1833, Wight moved to the Blue River settlement. Larry C. Porter and Ronald E. Romig, "The Prairie Branch, Jackson County Missouri: Emergence, Flourishing, and Demise, 1831–1834," *Mormon Historical Studies* 8, nos. 1–2 (Spring/Fall 2007):23. Personal names and branch locations are found in George A. Smith and Thomas Bullock, "A Partial List of the Persons Who Were Driven Out of Jackson County, Missouri, by the Mob in 1833," August 27, 1864, CHL, hereafter cited as "A Partial List."

34. Smith and Bullock, "A Partial List," 1–38.

35. *JSP*, R1:157, 96 [D&C 133:5; 45:68].

36. "A Prophecy Given to the Church of Christ, March 7, 1831," *The Evening and the Morning Star* 1, no. 1 (June 1832):2 [D&C 45:22].

37. "The Book of Mormon," *The Evening and the Morning Star* 1, no. 8 (January 1833): 59.

38. "The Elders in the Land of Zion to the Church of Christ Scattered Abroad," *The Evening and the Morning Star*, 1, no. 1 (July 1832):13; "The Elders Stationed in Zion to the Churches Abroad, in Love, Greeting," *The Evening and the Morning Star* 2, no. 14 (July 1833):110.

39. John Corrill, *A Brief History of the Church of Christ of Latter Day Saints* (St. Louis: by the Author, 1839), 19; also in *JSP*, H2:146.

40. *Missouri Intelligencer*, August 10, 1833, 2.

41. McCoy, "The Other Side," 9.

42. Corrill, *A Brief History of the Church of Christ of the Latter Day Saints*, 19; also in *JSP*, H2:146.

43. "The Elders Stationed in Zion to the Churches Abroad, in Love, Greeting," *The Evening and the Morning Star* 2, no. 14 (July 1833):110–111.

44. "The Elders Stationed in Zion to the Churches Abroad, in Love, Greeting," 110; McCoy, "A Famous Town," 8.

45. "Let Every Man Learn His Duty," *The Evening and the Morning Star* 1, no. 8 (January 1833):61 [D&C 85:7–8].

46. Oliver Cowdery to John Whitmer, January 1, 1834, Oliver Cowdery Letter Book, 1833–1838, 15, copy, CHL.

47. "From a conference of 12 High Priests to the Bishop, his Counsel and the inhabitants of Zion, Orson Hyde and Hyrum Smith," January 14, 1833, Kirtland Letter Book, 23, CHL. For a consideration of the Missouri problems, see Matthew C. Godfrey, "'Seeking after Monarchal Power and Authority': Joseph Smith and Leadership in the Church of Christ, 1831–1832," *Mormon Historical Studies* 13, no. 1–2 (Spring/Fall 2012):15–37.

48. *JSP*, R1:207–208 [D&C 78:3–4, 7–11]. D&C changed from original.

49. See Max H. Parkin, "Joseph Smith and the United Firm: The Growth and Decline of the Church's First Master Plan of Business and Finance, Ohio and Missouri, 1832–1834," *BYU Studies* 46, no. 3 (2007):5–66.

50. Frederick G. Williams. "Plan of the House of the Lord" for the Independence Temple, June 25, 1833, fd. 1, CHL; and Frederick G. Williams. "Plan of the House of the Lord," for the Independence Temple, ca. August 1833, MS 2568, fd. 2, CHL.

51. *JSP*, R1:246–248 [D&C 94]. The Kirtland House of the Lord was commenced June 5, 1833. The other two temples were planned but never built.

52. Joseph Smith to Beloved Brethren, August 6, 1833, Joseph Smith Papers, CHL.

53. *Missouri Intelligencer*, April 13, 1833, 1.

54. McCoy, "The Other Side," 9.

55. Alexander Majors, *Seventy Years on the Frontier* (Minneapolis, MN: Ross and Haines, 1965), 44–45.

56. Cited in Cannon and Cook, *Far West Record*, 63, n2.

57. McCoy, "A Famous Town," 8.

58. *Kansas City Journal*, June 5, 1881, 1.

59. *Missouri Intelligencer*, August 10, 1833, 2.

60. "Free People of Color," *The Evening and the Morning Star* 2, no. 14 (July 1833):109. Concerning the Mormons and slavery, Thomas Pitcher, head of the county militia said: "They did not interfere with the Negroes and we did not care whether they owned slaves or not." *Kansas City Journal*, June 19, 1881, 12.

61. *Missouri Intelligencer*, December 20, 1833, 2.

62. McCoy, "A Famous Town," 8.

63. "To His Excellency, Daniel Dunklin, Governor of the State of Missouri," *The Evening and the Morning Star* 2, no. 15 (December 1833):114–115. See also *Missouri Intelligencer*, August 10, 1833, 2.

64. Lydia Whiting petition in Johnson, *Mormon Redress Petitions*, 197, and 447–448.

65. Philo Dibble, "Philo Dibble's Narrative," in *Early Scenes in Church History: Eighth Book of the Faith-Promoting Series* (Salt Lake City: Juvenile Instructor Office, 1882), 82; reprinted in *Four Faith-Promoting Classics*, pt. 4 (Salt Lake City: Bookcraft, 1968), 82.

66. McCoy, "A Famous Town," 8.

67. Majors, *Seventy Years on the Frontier*, 47; Orrin Porter Rockwell petition in Johnson, *Mormon Redress Petitions*, 527–528.

68. Missouri Governor Daniel Dunklin later reprimanded Colonel Thomas Pitcher for depriving the Mormons of their guns. See *Missouri Intelligencer*, July 5, 1834, 2. Dunkin also ordered that the guns be returned to the Mormons. See Daniel Dunklin to Samuel D. Lucas, May 2, 1834, in *Times and Seasons* 6, no. 20 (January 1, 1846):1073–1074.

69. McCoy, "A Famous Town, 8; see also *Kansas City Journal*, February 16, 1879, 2.

70. Parley P. Pratt, *History of the Late Persecutions* (Detroit: Dawson and Bates, 1839), 20. Mormons said that Reverend Isaac McCoy participated with the mobs "and ordered men women and children to flee for their lives." "The Outrage in Jackson County, Missouri," *The Evening and the Morning Star* 2, no. 20 (May 1834):160; Orrin Porter Rockwell petition in Johnson, *Mormon Redress Petitions*, 526. McCoy stated that he rode with the mobs only "to regulate the conduct of the rash" and to prevent Mormons from "being beaten." Isaac McCoy, Journal, 1828–1834, November 5, 1833, Kansas State Historical Society, Topeka, Kansas.

71. Emily D. P. Young, "Autobiography," *Woman's Exponent* 13, no.18 (February 15, 1885):138; and Pratt, *History of the Late Persecutions*, 22.

72. Pratt, *History of the Late Persecutions*, 23.

73. Joseph Thorpe, *Early Days in the West* (Liberty, MO: Liberty Tribune, 1924), 76.

74. Orange Wight, "Recollections of Orange L. Wight," manuscript, 3, 1903, CHL.

75. Emily M. Austin, *Life among the Mormons* (Madison, WI: W. J. Cantwell, Book and Job Printer, 1882), 72–73.

76. W. W. Phelps to Dear Brethren, December 15, 1833, in *The Evening and the Morning Star* 2, no. 16 (January 1834):128.

77. Ibid.

78. *JSP*, R1:261 [D&C 101:2].

79. John Whitmer, "Day Book," 5, CHL.

80. Pratt, *Autobiography*, 107.

81. Thorpe, *Early Days in the West*, 76.

82. "A History, of the Persecution of the Church of Jesus Christ, of Latter Day Saints in Missouri," *Times and Seasons* 1, no. 4 (February 1840):50; also in *JSP*, H2:223–224.

83. *JSP*, R1:269 [D&C 101:86–88]; see also W. W. Phelps to Dear Brethren, February 27, 1834, in *The Evening and the Morning Star* 2, no. 18 (March 1834):139. See Lewis Cass to A. S. Gilbert, W. W. Phelps, E. Partridge, and others, May 2, 1834, in *Times and Seasons* 6, no. 20 (January 1, 1846): 1073.

84. See Algernon Sidney Gilbert to A. Leonard, February 13, 1834, in *Times and Seasons* 6, no. 15 (August 15, 1845): 992–993. The letter is incorrectly dated 1844; the correct date is 1834.

85. See Ray County, Missouri, Circuit Court Record, Book A, 249–250; Fifth Circuit Court, Jackson County, Record B, 282–285.

86. Daniel Dunklin to Colonel J. Thornton, June 6, 1834, in Joseph Smith Jr., *History of the Church of Jesus Christ of Latter-day Saints*, ed. B. H. Roberts, 2d ed., rev., 7 vols. (Salt Lake City: Deseret Book, 1971), 2:84–86 (hereafter referred to as *History of the Church*); and John Corrill to Brother O. Cowdery, *The Evening and the Morning Star* 2, no. 16 (January 1834):126

87. See *JSP*, R1:270–274 [D&C 103]; "Kirtland Council Minute Book," February 24, 1834, 42, CHL.

88. *Missouri Intelligencer*, June 7, 1834, 3.

89. Letter from an unnamed Missouri correspondent to his father in Mason County, Kentucky, June 20, 1834, published in the *Connecticut Courant*, August 4, 1834, n. p.

90. *History of the Church*, 2:102–105. Moses Martin recorded that the storm was "one of the most shocking storms ever known." Moses Martin, Journal, 9, CHL.

91. "Propositions, &c of the 'Mormons,'" *The Evening and the Morning Star* 2, no. 22 (July 1834):176; *Upper Missouri Enquirer*, July 2, 1834, n. p. The original documents contained a dozen signatures, CHL.

92. Letter from an unnamed Missouri correspondent to his father in Mason County, Kentucky, June 28, 1834, published in the *Connecticut Courant*, August 4, 1834, n. p. This letter was dated eight days after the first letter. See n89.

93. *JSP*, R1:284 [D&C 105:9, 13–14].

94. See Roger D. Launius, *Zion's Camp, Expedition to Missouri, 1834* (Independence, MO: Herald Publishing House, 1984), 145–152.

95. *History of the Church*, 2:123; Cannon and Cook, *Far West Record*, 70–72.

96. *JSP*, R1:284–287 [D&C 105:13, 16, 20, 27, 33].

97. Joseph Smith to Dear Brethren, Kirtland Letter Book, August 16, 1834, 85, CHL; *History of the Church*, 2:145.

98. *JSP*, R1:285 [D&C 105:23–24].

99. See "Clay County," in LaMar C. Berrett, ed. *Sacred Places, Volume 4: Missouri* (Salt Lake City, UT: Deseret Book, 2004), 161–219. The acreage owned by Mormons in Clay County was about forty percent more than Mormon land ownership in Jackson County.

100. *JSP*, H2:90. Two days before on September 22, 1835, Joseph Smith said to David Whitmer, "Behold, he it is, whom the Lord hath appointed to be captain of his host" to "go forth and build up the waste places of Zion." Patriarchal Blessing Book 1, 13, CHL.

101. Dean C. Jessee, Mark Ashurst-McGee, and Richard L. Jensen, eds., *Journals, Volume 1:1832–1839*, vol. 1 of the Journal series of *The Joseph Smith Papers*, eds. Dean C. Jessee, Ronald K. Esplin, and Richard Lyman Bushman (Salt Lake City: Church Historian's Press, 2008), 64, hereafter cited as *JSP*, J1.

102. *JSP*, J1:197.

103. In the 1981 and 2013 editions of the D&C, all code names were removed except the name used as a substitute for United Firm, namely United Order. See David J. Whitaker, "Substituted Names in the Published Revelations of Joseph Smith" *BYU Studies* 23, no. 1 (1983):

103–112; Parkin, "Joseph Smith and the United Firm," 58–59.

104. *JSP*, R1:287 [D&C 105:33]. For an account of some of the Missouri Church leaders receiving their endowment, see *JSP*, J1:212–216.

105. *JSP*, J1:212. After examining Joseph Smith's writings under this date, Dean C. Jessee concluded: "A contemporary revelation concerning their removal to Zion is not found in the pages that follow." Dean C. Jessee, *The Papers of Joseph Smith, Volume 2: Journal, 1832–1842* (Salt Lake City: Deseret Book Company, 1992), 204, n1.

106. *JSP*, J1:217 and n466.

107. *JSP*, H2:93; Cannon and Cook, *Far West Record*, 169.

108. Thorpe, *Early Days in the West*, 79.

109. "Public Meeting," *Latter Day Saints' Messenger and Advocate* 2, no. 11 (August 1836):354, 355.

110. "Public Meetings," *Latter Day Saints' Messenger and Advocate* 2, no. 11 (August 1836): 360.

111. Durward T. Stokes, "The Wilson Letters, 1835–1849," *Missouri Historical Review* 60, no. 4 (July 1966):504.

112. Drusilla Dorris Hendricks, "Historical Sketch," in *Women's Voices: An Untold History of the Latter-day Saints, 1830–1890*, ed. Kenneth W. Godfrey, Audrey M. Godfrey, and Jill Mulvay Derr (Salt Lake City: Deseret Book, 1982), 84.

113. Stokes, "The Wilson Letters," 507–509.

114. Edward Partridge, Journal, 1818–1836, May 1836, n. p., CHL.

115. *The Far West* (Liberty, MO), August 15, 1836, 1. John Murdock said that there were as many as two hundred families living near Crooked River waiting to find a permanent home. John Murdock, Journal, n. p., CHL.

116. "An Act to Organize Caldwell and Daviess counties," approved December 29, 1836, *Laws of the State of Missouri* (St Louis, MO: Chambers and Knapp, 1841), 46–47.

117. Cannon and Cook, *Far West Record*, 145–150; 162–171.

118. *JSP*, J1:258 [D&C 115:3]. On April 6, 1830, the official name of the Church was the "Church of Christ." In May 1834, it was changed to "The Church of the Latter Day Saints." See "The Saints," in *The Evening and the Morning Star* 2, no. 20 (May 1834):158. The name has remained the same since the April 1838 revelation with the exception of hyphenating Latter-day Saints.

119. *JSP*, J1:271 [D&C 116].

120. *JSP*, J1:288 [D&C 119:4].

121. *JSP*, J1:285 [D&C 118:6].

The 1838 Mormon-Missouri War: Historical Setting to the Hawn's Mill Tragedy

Gerrit Dirkmaat

In April 1839, having suffered for more than four months in Liberty Jail, Joseph Smith wrote an emotional letter to his wife, Emma. While looking through the grates of the lonesome prison, he wrote: "Dear and affectionate Wife, I have been under the grimace of a guard, night and day, and within the walls, grates, and screeking of iron doors, of a lonesome, dark, dirty prison. With emotions known only to God, do I write this letter, the contemplations of the mind under these circumstances, defies the pen, or tongue, or angels, to describe."

Of their impending trial, the Prophet wrote, "We lean on the arm of Jehovah, and none else, for our deliverance, and if he don't do it, it will not be done, you may be assured, for there is great thirsting for our blood, in this state; not because we are guilty of anything: but because . . . the mob party have sworn, to have our lives, at all hazards." He was eager to have his imprisonment, which he felt was the result of "false swearers," finally come to an end.

In closing, Joseph tenderly told his wife how greatly he missed her and the children: "My Dear Emma I think of you and the children continually. . . . I would gladly walk from here to you barefoot, and bareheaded, and half naked, to see you and think it great pleasure, and never count it toil."[1]

Joseph Smith's imprisonment was the result of what has often been referred to as the 1838 Mormon-Missouri War—a confused, sporadic, and at times brutally violent conflict. Unlike other confrontations, a number of the engagements did not even take place between official fighting forces but rather between vigilante groups, as local Missourians sought to illegally harass and expel the Mormons from their settlements—leading Mormons, in turn, to arm themselves for defense, and

It was April 4, 1839, when Joseph Smith penned the following to his wife Emma: "Dear and affectionate wife, Thursday night I sat down just as the sun is going down, as we peek through the grates of this lonesome prison, to write to you, that I may make known to you my situation." He had been away from his family for five months.

In his letter from Liberty Jail, Joseph said, "We cannot get into a worse hole than this is."

in some cases conduct their own retaliatory raids against their aggressors. At various times during the months of conflict, those involved believed the worst was behind them, that order had been restored, and that the conflict was essentially over. Though the hundreds of frightened Mormon families did not know it, the chaos would escalate from intermittent mob violence and harassment, culminating in the wholesale slaughter of seventeen men and boys at Hawn's Mill.

Joseph and Hyrum Smith and other Church leaders were subsequently arrested on charges stemming from the conflict, and they languished for months in jail, prompting Joseph's emotional letter to Emma. Significantly, the infamous "extermination order" issued by Missouri Governor Lilburn W. Boggs came near the end rather than at the beginning of the conflict. Boggs told the state militia that collectively, the Mormons "must be treated as enemies" and "exterminated"—in other words, "driven from the state, if necessary for the public peace."[2] The legacy of the conflict—house burnings, intimidation, armed conflict, and forced exodus—would psychologically traumatize thousands of Mormons for decades and would leave on the memory an indelible imprint of the hostilities they experienced.

SIGNS OF A GATHERING STORM

Although the actual conflict did not begin in earnest until late in the summer of 1838, signs of the gathering storm could be seen much earlier. By the summer of 1837, Mormons had begun settling in areas outside of Caldwell County—the county designated specifically for Mormon occupation—a situation that generated friction with their non-Mormon neighbors. In early July, W. W. Phelps, a member of the Missouri presidency, informed Church members in Kirtland that "our numbers increase daily." Phelps then ominously added that "public notice has been given by the *mob* in Davies[s] county, north of us, for the Mormons to leave that county by the first of August, and go into Caldwell."[3]

This was apparently no idle threat. Adam Black, a Daviess County justice of the peace, tried to enlist the support of other county officials in demanding that the Mormons leave the county. Black went to circuit court clerk James B. Turner to inform him that a number of citizens had concluded to meet with the Mormons and request that they leave the county peaceably. Turner demurred, telling Black that although he was "opposed to them as much as any man," he did not want to intervene, since it could jeopardize his chances for re-election.[4] Although nothing resulted, Black's plan to demand removal of the Mormons and Turner's response reflected the concerns of many Daviess County residents. The Mormon population in their county was growing, and they wanted that trend reversed. Black did not know it, but his actions in the summer of 1837 and his disposition against the Mormons would be a primary factor in the outbreak of hostilities a year later.

In 1837 and 1838, the Missourians had expected the Latter-day Saints to confine their settlements to Caldwell County, which had been created especially for them. Hence, when they began settling in other counties—such as Daviess County, where Lyman Wight had built a home—the old settlers took notice and were angry.

APOSTASY AND DISSENT IN OHIO AND MISSOURI

While tensions in nearby Daviess County simmered because of resentment against the growing number of Mormons in the region, the Mormons in Far West and Caldwell County were struggling with an entirely different problem—internal apostasy. In 1837, the Kirtland Safety Society Anti-Banking Company failed, causing a number of Church leaders and members to become disaffected from the Church. John F. Boynton, a member of the Quorum of the Twelve, attributed his difficulties to the failure of the bank, stating that "he had understood the Bank was instituted by the will of God, and he had been told that it never should fail let men do what they would."[5] The fraying fabric of the community in Kirtland among people who once professed the

Lyman Wight Cabin, *Daviess County, Missouri*; courtesy of the Church Archives, The Church of Jesus Christ of Latter-day Saints.

While tempers percolated in Missouri, troubles erupted for the Church in Kirtland. The failure of the Kirtland Safety Society angered many, especially some in prominent leadership positions, and resulted in apostasy and excommunications.

In April 1838, both Oliver Cowdery (below) and David Whitmer were excommunicated from the Church for apostasy and other charges. These actions grieved many in the Church in Far West and added to the roiling troubles that already existed there.

same beliefs was difficult to bear. Phoebe Woodruff, in a letter to her husband, Wilford, listed many of the most prominent members, including Book of Mormon witness Martin Harris, who had left the Church in Kirtland and had subsequently turned against it. Exasperated by the situation, she wrote, "O Wilford what is this world coming to[?] My heart almost shrinks within me when I look around on the state of things."[6] The growing legal and civil troubles facing Joseph Smith as a result of the bank failure forced him to leave Ohio and move to Far West to join the largest body of Saints in Missouri.

However, when Joseph Smith arrived at Far West on March 14, 1838, the Church there was experiencing a similar upheaval. Some of the dissension resulted from negative reports of the Prophet's dealings in Kirtland, as he explained upon his arrival: "Various & many have been the falsehoods written from thence to this place." But the primary issues in Far West stemmed from the excommunication of John Whitmer and W. W. Phelps over accusations of financial corruption, failure to submit to revelatory authority, and "unchristian like conduct." The hearing was held before the Far West high council, presided over by Thomas B. Marsh and David W. Patten, the two senior members of the Twelve. Whitmer and Phelps were cut off from the Church, in spite of objections from David Whitmer, president of the Church in Missouri, and Oliver Cowdery, assistant president of the Church.[7]

Oliver Cowdery's status in the Church had been in question for months. In September 1837, Joseph Smith had written to the Missouri Saints that Cowdery had "been in transgression," but held out hope that because of his position "he will yet humble himself & magnify his calling." However, if Cowdery persisted, Joseph continued, "the church will soon be under the necessity of raising their hands against him."[8] By January 1838, the estrangement was further fueled by news of the problems in Kirtland and by Cowdery's accusation of adultery against Joseph Smith. Upon learning that the Prophet and Sidney Rigdon were contemplating a move to Far West, Cowdery showed

Kirtland Safety Society Note, courtesy of the Church History Library. Oliver Cowdery © Ken Corbett; for more information, visit www.kencorbettart.com.

contempt in a letter written to his brother Warren, wherein Oliver indicated that if Smith and Rigdon did move there, "it will be my endeavor to seek a location for myself and friends some where else."[9] Within a month of the Prophet and Rigdon's arrival in Far West, Oliver Cowdery and David Whitmer were both excommunicated.[10]

Worried that the presence and activities of these and other dissenters would invite mob violence, many in Far West desired that these former members leave the area. John Corrill explained that "the dissenters kept up a kind of secret opposition to the presidency and church . . . and occasionally [spoke] against them, influence[d] the minds of the members against them, and occasionally correspond[ed] with their enemies abroad, and the church, it was said, would never become pure unless these dissenters were routed from among them. Moreover, if they were suffered to remain, they would destroy the church."[11]

On June 17, 1838, President Sidney Rigdon, first counselor in the First Presidency, preached a sermon in Far West that referred to Mormon dissenters as "salt that had lost its savor" and "good for nothing but to be cast out." There were those, like Sidney, who were sufficiently angry with the dissenters to make sure they were indeed cast out.

On June 17, 1838, Sidney Rigdon ratcheted up the tension when he preached a fiery sermon in which he condemned the dissenters as "salt that had lost its savor" and therefore "good for nothing but to be cast out." Meanwhile, several influential leaders in Far West banded together to form a group known as the Danites, a paramilitary organization designed to defend members of the Church from recurring mob violence and "to put to rights physically that which is not right, and to cleanse the Church of very great evils, . . . inasmuch as they cannot be put to rights by teaching & persuasions."[12] Samson Avard, the group's ringleader, drew up a missive directed at Oliver Cowdery, David Whitmer, John Whitmer, Lyman Johnson, W. W. Phelps, and several other dissenters, ordering them to vacate Far West in three days or "we will use the means in our power to cause you to depart, for go you shall."[13] Within a few days, "these men took warning, and soon they were seen bounding over the prairie like the scape Goat to carry off their own sins we have not seen them since, their influence is gone," George Robinson wrote.[14] While their influence might have been removed from Caldwell County, he also recorded that "it happened about these times that some excitement was raised in the adjoining Counties, that is Ray & Clay, against us, in consequence of the sudden departure of these wicked characters, of the apostates from this Church, into that vicinity, reporting false stories, and statements."[15]

MORMON EXPANSION IN NORTHERN MISSOURI

Despite growing tensions in the area and previous threats issued to the Mormons by mob forces in Daviess County in 1837, Joseph Smith was also faced with the reality of accommodating hundreds of new immigrants who planned to settle in Missouri over the course of the next several months. As a result, he undertook several measures to further expand Mormon settlement locations outside of Caldwell County. In May 1838, Joseph and Hyrum Smith led a surveying expedition to Daviess County, during which time he identified the location of Adam-ondi-Ahman, its name reflecting the ancient historical and religious importance of the site. Soon thereafter, Mormon settlers relocated to the region and on June 28, 1838, the Prophet organized a new stake of Zion there. Vinson Knight, the bishop at Adam-ondi-Ahman, estimated that by August there were "about 120 families of Mormons in that county and about 140 of the old inhabitants."[16] Another major expansion of Mormon settlement beyond Caldwell County occurred in the spring of 1838 when Joseph Smith was approached by land speculators looking to sell a number of town lots in the settlement community of DeWitt in Carroll County, not far from the mouth of the Grand River.[17] John Murdock explained that on June 23, 1838, "G[eorge] M. Hinkel & I Bought near one half of the town plot of DeWitt, Carroll Co. Mo. For $500 being so instructed of Br. Joseph the Prophet & high Council." The 130 or so lots provided another avenue for Mormon settlement, and in early July, Hinkle and Murdock both moved their families to DeWitt.[18] As Joseph Smith and Sidney Rigdon later explained, "The saints at the time were emigrating into the country in considerable numbers, and a portion of them stopped at DeWitt. Some purchased farms in the vicinity, others bought property in the town, and again by the middle of October there were as many as seventy families in DeWitt."[19]

The negative reaction of Carroll County residents was almost immediate, evidence that the anger over the expanding Mormon presence was not isolated to Daviess County. Only weeks after the first Mormon settlers arrived in DeWitt, "a committee sent by the mobbers of Carrollton, the co[unty] seat . . . came and ordered us to leave the county by the 7th of August," wrote John Murdock. On

In this letter from David Thomas to Joseph Smith, dated March 31, 1838, Thomas offered to sell "as good land is in the world" for the purpose of establishing a settlement for the Saints. This offer was accepted and became the Mormon community of DeWitt.

Letter from David Thomas to Joseph Smith, courtesy of The Joseph Smith Papers; for more information, visit http://josephsmithpapers.org/paperSummary/letter-from-david-thomas-31-march-1838?locale=eng&p=2.

September 20, the leaders returned, furious that the Mormons in DeWitt still had not left, gave them ten more days to evacuate, and informed the Mormons that if they were "not all away by that time they would exterminate us without regard to age or sex and throw our goods into the river."[20]

ELECTION-DAY SKIRMISH AT GALLATIN

The first outbreak of violence in northern Missouri in 1838 took place at Gallatin, the Daviess County seat, in connection with the August statewide elections. Whigs had hoped to carry the county in the elections even though Jacksonian Democrats had dominated the state for more than a decade. In the 1836 presidential election, the total number of votes in the state was only 18,332, and Democrat Martin Van Buren carried the state by just more than 3,500 votes. In 1838, with margins this small and narrowing statewide, plus national unrest over the failing economy tied to the Democratic Party, Whig candidates hoped to make inroads in northern Missouri's counties by courting the Mormon vote.[21] However, in spite of political efforts made by Whigs, the Mormons continued to side with the Democrats.

William Peniston, a frustrated Whig candidate for the Missouri state assembly, attempted to turn the simmering anti-Mormon sentiment to his advantage. Previous to the elections, Peniston had tried to lobby Lyman Wight, one of the earliest Mormon settlers in Daviess County, for the Mormon vote, but Wight reportedly rejected the politician's entreaties because of Peniston's known association with the mobocratic forces in the county. Earlier, when Wight questioned Peniston "about his former hostilities and his previous attempt to drive the saints from their homes; as well as many abusive things he had said," Peniston reported "that he never had any intention of driving them from their homes; he only tried to scare them, and if he could not, he intended to let them alone." Struggling to explain why he had made so many antagonistic public statements in relation to Mormonism, Peniston said he had been wrong and that "he had been deceived by false reports, without being acquainted with the people; and, since he had become a acquainted with them, he found that they were first rate citizens." Unimpressed, Wight left Peniston's home knowing that the Mormons in the county would likely all vote against him.[22]

On August 6, 1838, a small group of Latter-day Saints went to Gallatin, Missouri, the county seat of Daviess County, to vote in local elections. When angry anti-Mormons sought to prevent the Mormons from voting, a fight broke out. Mormon John Lowe Butler picked up a large club and waded into the fray to defend his brethren. The power of rumor would make this minor dust-up far worse in consequences than the original event ever was.

Gallatin Brawl by Kelly Donovan.

If Peniston could not carry the Mormon vote, he hoped at least to suppress it. On August 6, 1838, as men from the county gathered to vote at the polls in Gallatin, he climbed atop a barrel and "called on the citizens and made a long speech, abusing the Mormons all that he could and said that he had been to drive the Mormons and he would do it again."[23] John Corrill reported that when Peniston saw that the Mormons were not going to vote for him, he "made a flaming speech . . . [and] said, that the Mormons ought not to be suffered to vote."[24] As the Mormons pressed forward to vote, members of the angry crowd began to push forward and eventually attack them. The Mormons and their antagonists used clubs, boards, knives, and shards of broken pottery in the melee that ensued.[25] While several were injured on both sides of the fracas, no mortal wounds were inflicted.

The first reports that reached Far West the next day were greatly exaggerated. Joseph Smith was told that "some two or three of our brethren were killed in consequence of the Malignity of the Missourians . . . and that, the men who were killed were left upon the ground and not suffered to be interred." This appalling yet incorrect report was coupled with information that the ballot violence was just the beginning, "that the majority of the county were determined to drive the brethren from the county."[26]

OPERATION ADAM BLACK

An expedition was immediately organized to go to Gallatin to investigate and to recover the bodies. Samson Avard, the leader of the Danites, set out with "some 15 or 20 men."[27] Joseph Smith, Hyrum Smith, Sidney Rigdon, and dozens of others soon followed. When Smith's company arrived at the home of Lyman Wight, about three miles from Gallatin, "we learned the truth concerning the said affray, which had been considerably exaggerated, yet, there had been a serious Outrage committed."[28] Though no Mormons had in fact been killed and left lying in the street, the reports confirmed that Mormons had been prevented by mob violence from voting.

Fearing that the election-day violence in Gallatin would simply be used as a pretext by Adam Black to renew his efforts to oust Mormons from the county entirely, the Mormon expeditionary force determined to visit Black and get him to agree to uphold the law. Not only had Black's previous actions aroused the suspicion that he was involved in foul play, reports were already circulating that he was planning to lead a retaliatory strike against the Mormon settlement at Adam-ondi-Ahman. Joseph Smith explained that such reports were taken seriously, since just a few months earlier Black had been engaged in endeavoring to drive the Mormons from Daviess County, having "personally

Ordered" several Mormons to leave despite having no legal grounds to do so. In order to ascertain the truth of these reports, Joseph Smith "dispatched a committee to . . . know what [Black's] intentions were, and as we understood he was a peace Officer, we wished to know what we might expect from him." This initial group returned shortly, having been insulted and rebuffed, so the Prophet decided to accompany a larger body of Mormon men to meet with Black again. After Samson Avard and a few others failed to convince Black to sign an agreement that he would deal justly with the Mormons, Joseph Smith visited him personally and reported that he was "quite hostile in his feelings toward the Mormons." However, Black eventually signed a statement affirming "that he did not belong to the mob, neither would he take any part with them, but said he was bound by his oath to support the Constitution of the United States."[29] Having secured a signed statement repudiating any intended malfeasance, the Mormons left.

However, no sooner had the Mormon force departed than Adam Black hurried away to Richmond to swear out a statement denouncing the Mormon delegation and accusing them of threatening his life if he did not sign the aforementioned statement. He declared that the Mormons had "threatened the lives of myself & other individuals, and did say they intended to make every citizen of said County sign such [an] obligation." In Black's version of events, a force of 154 armed Mormons had coerced him to sign a document of which he did not approve, and they did it on the "penalty of instant death."[30] For his part, Joseph Smith swore to the effect that "no violence was offered to any individual, in his presence or within his knowledge."[31]

Nevertheless, the fact that an armed group of Mormons had crossed over from Caldwell to Daviess County and then surrounded the home of a justice of the peace in what appeared to be a show of force and intimidation became a rallying point for anti-Mormon forces

Judge Adam Black escalated the anger of his fellow Missourians against the Mormons when he swore in this affidavit that Joseph Smith and others had "threatened him with instant death" if he did not sign a promise not to further molest the Saints.

Adam Black Affidavit, courtesy of the Missouri State Archive.

Judge Adam Black's vitriolic accusations about threats from the Mormons fueled the fires of hatred against the Saints. In response to Black's false statements, Joseph Smith swore out an affidavit certifying that "no violence was offered to any individual, in his presence or within his knowledge."

throughout the county and the surrounding region. If the goal had been to have Black on record as not supporting the mobocratic forces in Daviess County, the end was not achieved by the encounter. Instead, Black renounced the agreement he had signed as having been done under duress, and he noised abroad the treacherous and violent intentions of the Mormons, stoking the fires of animosity.

Still, in the immediate aftermath of the election-day violence, some more rationally minded citizens in Daviess County sought to extinguish rather than fan the flames. On August 8–9, a group of Daviess residents and elected officials met with the Mormon leaders in an effort to "sue for peace." The contingent was aptly led by John Williams, the victorious Democratic candidate who had defeated William Peniston for the Missouri House seat. For reasons that were certainly political as well as peaceful, Williams sought to contain the possible repercussions of the nasty election-day affair. Also among the group was James B. Turner—who, the year before, had for political reasons refused to help Black drive the Mormons from Daviess.[32] At the end of the meeting the two groups agreed to "preserve each others rights, and stand in their defense," and "all offenders [were] to be dealt with according to the law and Justice."[33]

Adam Black's reports in Ray County persuaded Circuit Court Judge Austin A. King to issue an arrest warrant for both Joseph Smith and Lyman Wight. However, when the sheriff of Daviess County attempted to arrest Joseph Smith, the sheriff assured Joseph that he would not be tried in Daviess County given the hostile attitude of the citizens there. In any case, the sheriff was outside of his jurisdiction in Caldwell County and therefore Smith refused to submit.[34]

Lyman Wight was another matter altogether. Since Wight lived in Daviess County, the local sheriff had the authority to arrest him, but apparently decided against it after a determined and boisterous Wight resisted. These initial failures to bring the Mormon leaders to justice further fanned the flames of those seeking to indict the Mormons as lawbreakers and threats to the community.

Black also called for volunteers from the surrounding counties to help "resist" the Mormons. Significantly, Hiram Comstock—a resident of Livingston County who later participated in the attack at Hawn's Mill—organized a committee that raised two hundred men to march to Daviess and fight the Mormons. He also tried to raise an additional force through a public pronouncement in nearby Carroll County, where the Mormons in DeWitt were arriving under increasing pressure.[35]

REPORTS OF A MORMON-INDIAN LEAGUE

On September 1, several men from Brunswick, Chariton County, wrote Governor Lilburn Boggs regarding the threat the Mormons posed to the state. The men explained to the governor that "there is a deeply laid scheme existing among these fanatics, that will be highly destructive in character, & at once subversive to the rights & liberties of the people." On top of the threat of violence that the Mormons appeared to pose, the writers claimed that "their people are taught to believe & expect that immense numbers of Indians of various tribes are only waiting the signal for a general rise, when, as they state it, the flying or destroying Angel will go through the land, & work the general destruction of all that are not Mormons."[36] Only a few days later, John N. Sapp, claiming to have been a former Mormon and Danite, added greater weight to this charge, also claiming that the Mormons were attempting to "induce the Indians to Join them (the said Mormons) in making war upon the Missourians and that they Expected to be fully prepared to commence war this fall or next spring at fartherest [sic]."[37] Having the Mormons charged with inciting the Indians to violence played on both the racial animosity of white Americans toward Indians and the ever-present fear of attacks among frontier communities. Charges of this nature were calculated to whip up public sentiment even more decidedly against the Mormons.

Yet even before these letters carrying the threat of Indian-Mormon violence reached the governor, Boggs had issued orders that the state militia be turned out in consequence of possible Indian violence, suggesting that rumors of this nature had already reached his desk. Because of the Indian threat and "the recent civil disturbances in the

Missouri Circuit Court Judge Austin A. King issued an arrest warrant for Lyman Wight in connection with the Adam Black incident. When Wight refused to submit to the sheriff, Missourians were further incited against the Mormons, who were already seen as fanatical lawbreakers.

Counties of Caldwell, Daviess and Carroll," the militia was to march north and maintain the peace.[38]

SEPTEMBER DISTURBANCES IN DAVIESS

Arriving with his state troops in Far West on September 3, Major-General David R. Atchison's encounter with the Mormons proved amiable. Not only did Atchison agree that the Mormons were the ones who had been wronged, he agreed to "do all in his power to disperse the mob." Furthermore, he and Brigadier General Alexander Doniphan agreed to serve as defense attorneys for Joseph Smith and Lyman Wight in the forthcoming September 7 trial before Judge Austin King in Daviess County on the earlier charges stemming from the alleged threats made against Adam Black. Ironically, William Peniston, whose anti-Mormon tirade had incited the election-day violence, served as the prosecuting attorney, with Adam Black as his only witness. After hearing the case, Judge Austin A. King made no ruling but bound the trial over to the next term of the circuit court and allowed Joseph Smith and Lyman Wight to go free after posting bonds as security.[39] Vinson Knight recalled that following the trial and arrival of the troops, "we thought that the matter was settled and we all went about our business."[40]

When news of the trial reached the editors of the *Western Star*, a Ray County newspaper, they surmised that "a very different face has been placed upon" the Adam Black affair than the one Black had so publicly claimed. The paper further concluded that the trial "completely stamped Black, Comstock, and others with falsehood." Although the trial should have put an end to the growing calls against the Mormons, the report noted that the non-Mormon citizens of Daviess County had been busily engaged trying to elicit support from surrounding counties to form an armed mob and drive the Mormons out of Daviess. In the face of this threat, the Mormons were arming in preparation to defend themselves.[41]

Following the trial, Atchison's force departed Far West, expecting that the outcome of the trial would placate the mobocratic forces in the area, but tensions only increased. On September 9, Mormon officials in Caldwell County apprehended three men trying to smuggle stolen guns from Ray County through Caldwell to Daviess to bolster the gathering mob forces there. The men were legally arrested and arraigned in Far West, but anti-Mormon forces believed the Mormons had taken the men as hostages and considered Mormon actions to have been hostile. A militia detachment under the command of Alexander

Lilburn W. Boggs served as governor of Missouri from 1836 to 1840. Before he ever issued his infamous extermination order of October 27, 1838, Governor Boggs called up the state's militia to put down the Mormons solely on the strength of rumors he had heard.

Opposite Top: Major-General David Rice Atchison of the Missouri State Militia was the commanding officer of the forces called out by Governor Boggs. When he arrived at Far West, he concluded that it was the Mormons who had been wronged, and he offered to do all in his power to disperse the mobs.

Opposite Bottom: With the threats of the mobs, the citizens of DeWitt appealed to Governor Boggs by this petition, outlining the events and asking for his help, saying, "We therefore pray you to take such steps as shall put a stop to all lawless proceedings." The governor ignored the request.

Doniphan returned to Far West to take charge of the prisoners and to take custody of the guns. In the meantime, vigilante forces in Daviess County were becoming increasingly more aggressive.[42]

EXPULSION OF THE MORMONS FROM DEWITT

Although Atchison's and Doniphan's troops temporarily forestalled any general assault on the Mormons living in Daviess and Caldwell counties, tensions surrounding DeWitt in Carroll County were only escalating.[43]

The Mormons there sought protection from Governor Boggs against the gathering storm. They explained that on September 20 they had been assailed by "one hundred to one hundred and fifty armed men & threatened with force & violence to drive certain peaceable citizens from their homes in defiance of all law & threatened them to drive said citizens out of the county, but on deliberation concluded to give them . . . till the first of October next to leave said County, & threatened if not gone by that time to exterminate them without regard to age or sex."[44]

The Mormons were not the only ones reporting the renewed threats and violence surrounding DeWitt. A committee sent from Chariton County to see why the Carroll County residents were calling people to arms against the Mormons in DeWitt sent a troubling message to Governor Boggs on October 5. They found that the mob surrounding the town had no specific grievance at all against the Mormons except that they were living in the county. The mobocratic forces derided the Mormons as outsiders, adding that the

Major-General David Rice Atchison, courtesy of Alexander L. Baugh. Citizens of DeWitt Petition, courtesy of the Missouri State Archive.

Mobs assembled against the small Latter-day Saint community of DeWitt and forced the people out for no other reason than that they were Mormons. The citizens of DeWitt appealed to the governor, but he callously declared that the Mormons and the mobs would have to "fight it out."

mobocrats "are unwilling for them to remain there, which is the cause of their waging . . . a war of extermination, or remove them from the said county. We also went into DeWitt, to see the situation of the Mormons, we found them in the act of defense, begging for peace, and wishing for the civil authorities to repair there as early as possible to settle the difficulties between the parties. Hostilities have commenced and will continue, until they are stopped by the civil authorities."[45] Those hostile actions included random gunshots being fired at homes and in the direction of the Mormon settlers in and around DeWitt.

Governor Boggs was also learning more from authoritative sources about the mob's advances on DeWitt. General Hiram G. Parks, in a letter to Boggs on October 7, asked the governor for more troops in order to "have a force sufficient to manage these belligerents. Should these troops arrive here in time, I hope to be able to prevent Bloodshed nothing seems so much in demand here (to hear the Carroll County men talk) as Mormon scalps." Though Parks believed the Mormons in the area had done nothing wrong and were only defending themselves, he forwarded on to the governor his "settled opinion, [that] the Mormons will have no rest until they leave; whether they will or not, time only can tell."[46]

General Parks had hoped he would be given more troops to help head off the conflict, but Boggs was unresponsive. Meanwhile, General

Siege of DeWitt by C. C. A. Christensen, courtesy of the Church History Library.

David R. Atchison made the fateful decision to prize pragmatism over principle. He ordered Parks to do what he could to disperse the forces, but above all prevent any more armed Mormons from coming to the aid of DeWitt. He explained to Boggs in a letter that he had "also suggested to Parks, to urge it upon the Mormons in Carroll County, to sell out and remove elsewhere."[47] Although the only basis for the assault on the Mormons residing in DeWitt was their religious affiliation, Atchison realized that the salient Mormon community could not survive indefinitely, surrounded as it was by hostile forces that grew larger by the day. Though the Mormons had purchased their lands legally, they were being ordered to leave because of who they were and what they believed, not because of some alleged transgression against the wider community. Even John Corrill, who was critical of Mormon actions during the Mormon War and who later left the Church, explained: "I never heard of any accusation that the people of Carroll had against the Mormons, but still they were determined they should not settle in that county."[48]

Joseph Smith had personally come to DeWitt with a small relief force on October 6 to assess the grave situation. He explained:

> We thought it necessary to send immediately to the Governor, to inform him of the circumstances; hoping, from the Executive, to receive the protection which we needed, and which was guaranteed to us, in common with other citizens. Several Gentlemen of standing and respectability, who lived in the immediate vicinity, who were not in any wise connected with the church of Latter Day Saints, who had witnessed the proceedings of our enemies; came forward and made affidavits to the treatment we had received, and concerning our perilous situation; and offered their services to go and present the case to the Governor themselves. A messenger was accordingly despatched [sic] to his Excellency, who made known to him our situation. But instead of receiving any aid whatever, or even sympathy from his Excellency, we were told that "the quarrel was between the Mormons and the mob," and that "we might fight it out."[49]

Facing growing threats and actual violence near DeWitt, a governor's office that appeared entirely unwilling to help, and a state militia whose officials were actually encouraging them to give in to the intimidation and terror of the lawless, Mormon leaders decided to give in and abandon DeWitt. Without any support from state officials, it would have

The Prophet Joseph Smith heard of the siege in DeWitt and journeyed in secret by way of back roads to help the Saints there. With no hope of relief, it was October 11, 1838, when Joseph assisted them in abandoning the community. Several Saints of DeWitt lost their lives as a result of the inhumanity of mobs.

been only a matter of time before the mobocratic forces—who by this time had secured a cannon—had grown in strength to a point that they could make a direct assault on DeWitt rather than just on the outlying areas. On October 11, the Mormons in DeWitt began evacuating their homes and lands and made a difficult trek to Far West, harassed by mob forces and suffering from "fatigue and privations."[50]

While the Adam Black affair in Daviess had allowed many Missourians to claim moral authority for the harassment of Mormons in Daviess County, the blatant xenophobia exhibited in Carroll County, entirely free from justifiable antecedent, turned several Missouri newspapers against the mob forces. By late September the *Columbia Patriot* had already concluded that there was "neither cause nor justification" for the mob actions taken against the Mormons. The paper surmised that the Mormons were not the aggressors and in fact had "been most vilely slandered." In the editor's opinion, there was no justification for gathering a mob because of salty sermons from Sidney Rigdon or preposterous claims that the Mormons should be allowed to settle only in Caldwell County: "Wherever, in this wide land, the government, or individuals will choose to sell a man land there he has the right to go, reside and remain free unmolested, so long as he does not infringe the laws, be he Hottentot or Christian, Islamite or Mormon." The *Patriot* believed that an attempt to acquire Mormon lands superseded presumed community interests, and that the mob forces "think by raising an outcry against them and exciting them to violence they may be driven off and their lands be portioned out to other hands."[51] The *St. Louis Republican* also concluded that the Mormons were the "injured party, and that the statements of Justice Black and others . . . were entirely false and groundless."[52]

Not even did the peaceful Mormon capitulation and appeasement in DeWitt allay tensions among mob forces. Rather, the victory only emboldened them. An exasperated Major-General Atchison wrote Governor Boggs that although the Mormons had left DeWitt and therefore settled the tensions in Carroll County, "a portion of the men from Carroll County, with one piece of artillery, are on their march for Daviess County, where it is thought the same lawless game is to be played over, and the Mormons to be driven from that county, and probably from Caldwell County: nothing in my opinion but the strongest measures within the power of the Executive will put down this spirit of Mobocracy." Atchison explained that Parks had been unable to dispel the mob forces surrounding DeWitt because his militiamen were sympathetic to the mob and therefore would not take a forceful stand against them. Atchison reminded Boggs that the Mormon conflict had been "in a high degree ruinous to the people and disgraceful to the State. I would again respectfully suggest strong measures to put down this spirit of mob, and misrule, or permit them to fight it out, if your Excellency should conclude the latter expedient best calculated to produce quiet and restore order, issue an order to [me] to discharge the troops now engaged in that service." If the governor was not going to authorize strong measures against the mob forces, having militiamen under arms was not only costly to the state but actually could have fueled the violence if the men—like those under the command of General Parks—sided with the mob in dereliction of their duty.[53]

MORMON OFFENSIVE IN DAVIESS COUNTY

Arriving with the DeWitt refugees back in Far West and Adam-ondi-Ahman, Joseph Smith and other Church leaders faced a seemingly no-win scenario. By this time the mobs in Carroll County were converging on Daviess, emboldened by their successful eviction of Mormons from DeWitt. Meanwhile, reports of isolated acts of violence against Mormon settlements were arriving daily in Far West. Even Major-General Atchison understood that the mob would repeat the same battle plan—harass outlying Mormon settlements, surround Mormon settlements in Daviess County, and demand their removal. If the Mormons did nothing, the growing mob forces stationed in the mob-friendly areas of Daviess County would continue to grow in strength. The Mormons, prevented by state militia troops from reinforcing their positions as they had been in DeWitt, would eventually become exposed to an assault they could not withstand and would have to again retreat. John Corrill reported that following Joseph Smith's return from DeWitt, news arrived that Mormon prisoners had been taken by the mob forces and that a cannon was en route to Daviess. The mob leaders claimed that they would "drive the Mormons from Davies to Caldwell, and from Caldwell to h—l."

In this letter dated October 16, 1838, Major-General David Rice Atchison stated to the governor, "Nothing in my opinion but the strongest measures within the power of the Executive will put down this spirit of mobocracy." He further described the actions of the mob to that point as "ruinous to the people and disgraceful to the State." Notwithstanding these urges from his commanding officer in the field, the governor did nothing.

General David Rice Atchison Letter, courtesy of the Missouri State Archive.

Joseph Smith despaired that the Mormons "had been driven from place to place; their property destroyed; their rights as citizens taken from them; abuse upon abuse practiced upon them from time to time; they had sought for redress through the medium of the law, but never could get it; the State of Missouri refused to protect them in their rights; the executive had been petitioned many times, but never would do anything for them."[54]

Given that events in DeWitt had made it clear to Mormon leaders that there was no appeasing the anti-Mormon mob, Church leaders made the fateful decision to proactively deprive the mob of their bases of operations in Daviess County and punish the mob-supporting citizens there before mob forces could reassemble in great numbers. This show of force would hopefully deprive the mob of some supplies, especially stockpiled guns the mob could use in a future assault on Adam-on-di-Ahman, as well as assert to anti-Mormon forces and sympathizers that the Mormons would no longer be pushed. Corrill explained that the armed expedition "meant to make clean work now, and expel the mob from Davies[s] and then from Caldwell county." Confronted by Mormons in the form of the Caldwell County militia, the Mormons reasoned that the mob forces "when they found they would have to fight, would not be so fond of gathering together against them."[55]

However, Mormon militia raids into Daviess from Caldwell backfired, since the show of force only succeeded in providing the anti-Mormon forces the catalyst they had been looking for to justify an all-out assault on Mormon positions and turn the "neutral" state militia decidedly against the Mormons. Mormon forces looted and then burned four homes and businesses in Gallatin, where the election-day fight had sparked the conflict between the two groups. In the slightly larger village of Millport, more than a dozen homes and businesses were again deprived of their valuable contents and then burned. This punitive expedition into Daviess County also succeeded in capturing a store of guns, as well as the cannon that had been sent from the

The Latter-day Saints knew that the mobs that had driven them from DeWitt were now bound for Adam-ondi-Ahman in Daviess County. They therefore opted for a preemptive strike and drove the mob element out of Daviess County. Though they had little choice to do otherwise, it proved to be a disastrous move, as it cost them the moral high ground in the court of public opinion. In this letter to the governor written by William Peniston, an avowed anti-Mormon driven from Daviess County, he decries the actions of the Mormons and pleads with the governor to "restore us to our lost homes."

DeWitt siege, but the extralegal depredations against supposed and known mob organizers and sympathizers allowed anti-Mormon forces to reclaim the moral initiative somewhat forfeited at DeWitt.

Among the Daviess County citizens targeted by the Mormon raiders was, not surprisingly, William Peniston, the Whig politico who had urged the crowd in Gallatin to prevent the Mormons from voting in the August election. The Penistons, a founding family of Millport, were targeted as a consequence of their support of the anti-Mormon mob. Peniston, among several other Daviess County residents, petitioned the governor for help and in an exaggerated tone informed him that Mormons had "plundered or robbed and burned every house in Gallatin, our County seat, among the rest our Post Office [and] have driven almost every individual from the County." More particularly, and more personally, he told the commander-in-chief with xenophobic flare, "They have burned for me two houses. . . . These facts are made known to you, sir, hoping that your authority will be used to stop the [outrages] of this banditti of Canadian refugees and restore us to our lost homes."[56]

While displaced Daviess County residents stoked the anti-Mormon fires in the surrounding counties, especially Ray and Livingston counties, Major-General Atchison's initial reaction is evidence that the Mormons felt justified in taking the offensive, and now both sides were guilty of wrongdoing. In a letter to Governor Boggs, Atchison explained that the situation had deteriorated: "The Mormons have become desperate and act like mad men, they have burned a store in Gallatin, they have burnt Millport, they have it is said plundered several houses and have taken away the arms from Diverse Citizens of that county. A cannon that was employed in the siege of DeWitt in Carroll County, and taken for a like purpose to Daviess County, has fallen into the hands of the Mormons, it is also reported that the anti-Mormons have when opportunity offered disarmed the Mormons, and burnt several of their houses."

Atchison explained that he could not be the one to decide which party was most at fault. Because the Mormons had started fighting

Major-General Atchison penned this letter to Governor Boggs on October 22, 1838; in it he acknowledged the desperation of the Mormons in their attack on the Daviess County settlers. However, notwithstanding the defensive actions of the Mormons, Atchison considered it a disgrace to himself and to the state for the soldiers under his command to act the part of a mob and drive the Mormons from the county.

Major-General Atchison Letter, courtesy of the Missouri State Archive.

It was during this difficult period that Thomas B. Marsh, president of the Quorum of the Twelve Apostles, went to Richmond and swore out this affidavit. Among other things, he said the following: "I have heard [Joseph] say that he should yet tread down his enemies, and walk over their dead bodies . . . and that he would make it one gore of blood from the Rocky Mountains to the Atlantic Ocean." Such inflammatory misrepresentations were caught up by the Missourians and greatly exacerbated the existing panic.

back against their opponents, he was "convinced that nothing short of driving the Mormons from Daviess County will satisfy the party opposed to them, and this I have not the power to do as I conceive legally." He continued: "There are no troops at this time in Daviess County; nor do I deem it expedient to send any there. For I am well convinced that it would but make matters worse, for Sir I do not feel disposed to disgrace myself, or permit the troops under my command to disgrace the State, and themselves, by acting the part of a mob." Atchison clearly feared the same kind of mutinous reaction on the part of his own troops if he were to march them into Daviess to play a neutral role, as General Parks had done at DeWitt; and he wanted no part of allowing his troops to help illegally drive the Mormons from Daviess County. He planned no grand retaliation for the Mormons' raid into Daviess County and their burning of Millport and homes in Gallatin, but remained content to let the matter play itself out. He closed the letter by telling Boggs he would follow orders, but he personally maintained that "if the Mormons are to be drove from their homes let it be done without any color of law, and in open defiance thereof; let it be done by volunteers acting upon their own responsibilities."[57]

Once again, the situation would be exacerbated by dissension within the Mormon hierarchy. Several leading men, perhaps fearing that the full weight of the state militia would now fall against them after the burning of Millport and Gallatin, expressed their disapproval of recent events, turned against Joseph Smith, and began to circulate reports of Mormon treachery. Most notable was the disaffection of Thomas B. Marsh, president of the Quorum of the Twelve. In late October he left Far West and went to Richmond, where he issued a lengthy affidavit stating that Mormon leaders intended to burn Buncombe, Richmond, and Liberty if the

Thomas B. Marsh Affidavit, courtesy of the Missouri State Archive.

citizens of any of those communities made any movements against the Mormons. In fact, in Marsh's jaded view, there was no satiating Joseph Smith's thirst for conquest. He attested that Smith planned to not only violently take over the entire state of Missouri, but also "the U.S. & ultimately the whole world."[58] Orson Hyde, also a member of the Twelve, validated a number of Marsh's claims in an affidavit of his own.[59]

GOVERNOR BOGGS INTERVENES

While Atchison was willing to remain aloof from the unfolding violence, Boggs was not. On October 23, more than a dozen citizens in Richmond wrote the governor requesting that he intervene in the hostilities. "All the inhabitants of Daviess county have left, and sought refuge in Livingston or this [Ray] county," they wrote. "It is the desire of the citizens that his Excellency would visit this section of country and call out a sufficient number of troops to put a stop to the further ravages, [for] if such measures are not taken shortly, the whole country will be overrun."[60] On October 26, after receiving this and other reports, the governor decided to take definitive military measures against the Mormons and ordered the call-up of five divisions, each consisting of four hundred men (two thousand total), to rendezvous at Richmond, at which time they would use military force to restore homes and property to the expelled citizens of Daviess County.[61] Sadly, when the Mormons had made a similar application during the siege of DeWitt, Boggs had turned a deaf ear.

Orson Hyde, a member of the Quorum of the Twelve Apostles, signed Thomas B. Marsh's affidavit. By the following year, Hyde sought out Church leaders (now in Illinois), recanted his statements, and asked to be reinstated to full fellowship. He was forgiven and reinstated to his place in the Twelve.

BATTLE OF CROOKED RIVER

Significantly, the day before Boggs called for full-scale military intervention, the most significant clash of the entire Mormon War had already occurred. Captain Samuel Bogart, a Methodist preacher serving as the leader of a small company of Ray County militia, had been allowed to patrol the border between Ray and Caldwell counties, ostensibly to prevent any Mormon incursions into Ray similar to the forays into Daviess.[62] Bogart's actions, though, clearly reveal that his intentions were far from benign and defensive. During his reconnaissance, his troops ordered several Mormon families out of their homes, threatened some with death if they did not leave, and even beat one Mormon man, taking him and two others hostage.

Battle of Crooked River by C. C. A. Christensen, courtesy of the Church History Library.

It was October 25, 1838, at a place called Crooked River when Mormon militia under the command of Apostle David W. Patten clashed violently with Missouri militia forces. When the battle was over, four men lay dead and fifteen wounded. Once again, the outcome of this conflict would be wildly inflated by far-flung rumor.

When news of Bogart's actions reached Far West, Mormon officials in Caldwell—assuming that Bogart was at the head of a vigilante force intent on infiltrating the Mormon county—called out a contingent of their own county militia, composed entirely of Mormons and led by David W. Patten of the Quorum of the Twelve. Hearing that Bogart and his men were camped south of Far West on Crooked River, Patten's company set out around midnight on October 24 to find the enemy force and rescue the three men. Early on the morning of October 25, as the Mormon company approached Bogart's encampment, one of the sentinels standing guard opened fire, mortally wounding the Mormon guide, eighteen-year-old Patterson O'Banion. Finding Bogart's men in a protected position on the banks of the Crooked River, Patten ordered a frontal charge against their enemy's position. By the time the smoke cleared, Bogart's Ray County militia had been routed and scattered, leaving nearly their entire baggage train to be confiscated by the Mormon troops. The Ray County militia suffered six wounded and one killed, while the Mormons, who had charged the position, fared worse. Gideon Carter was killed and nine other men were wounded, some critically. Patterson O'Banion and David W. Patten died a few hours later from their wounds, bringing the Mormon death toll to three.[63]

While the victory over Bogart's forces at Crooked River temporarily ended armed intimidation of Mormons in southern Caldwell County, the consequences for the Mormons in Missouri were dire. Governor Boggs—who had already decided to call out the state militia against the Mormons on October 26 before hearing of the Battle of Crooked River—received wildly exaggerated casualty reports from the battle, including information that the Mormons were marching on Richmond to burn it. One report claimed that "Capt Bogard [Bogart] and all his company amounting to between fifty and sixty were massacred by the Mormons at Buckhorn twelve miles north of Richmond except three." This grossly overstated dispatch assured readers that "this statement you may rely on as being true."⁶⁴ A much tamer communiqué nevertheless reported to Governor Boggs that the Mormons had defeated Bogart, "killing some ten men, wounding many others and taking the most of the remainder prisoners." The informants continued: "Many of the Mormons having been killed in the fight as is supposed. We have but little hope from these wretched desperadoes, but that they will kill all these prisoners."⁶⁵

EXTERMINATION ORDER

Without taking the time to investigate the inflated reports of Mormon atrocities and violations of the law, Boggs made the fateful decision to strengthen his October 26 order and called for total Mormon submission, surrender, and expulsion. On October 27, after receiving reports of the Crooked River Battle, the governor wrote to General John B. Clark that the new information "entirely changes the face of things and places the Mormons in the attitude of an open and armed defiance of the laws." He accused the Latter-day Saints collectively of having "made war upon the people of this State." As a result, Boggs coldly instructed General Clark that because the Mormons' "outrages are beyond all description,"

After hearing grossly skewed reports on the atrocities of the Mormons, Governor Lilburn W. Boggs issued Executive Order 44, otherwise known as "The Extermination Order." In it he ordered, "The Mormons must be treated as enemies and must be exterminated or driven from the State if necessary for the public peace. Their outrages are beyond all description."

On October 31, 1838, Joseph Smith and others were betrayed into the hands of the Missourians, were arrested, and were taken south to Independence. After a hearing, they spent five months in the jail at Liberty, Clay County, Missouri. Meanwhile, the rest of the Mormons, true to the governor's orders, were driven from the state.

they "must be treated as enemies and must be exterminated or driven from the State if necessary for the public peace."[66] The "Extermination Order" and the marshalling of state militia forces against the Mormons as enemies of the state—the strategy of anti-Mormons like Adam Black and William Peniston to drive the Saints permanently from their homes in Daviess County—became the official policy of the state of Missouri.

On October 31, Joseph Smith was arrested and taken into custody; three days later, on November 2, Mormon leaders officially surrendered to state militia officials. In the days and weeks ahead, Caldwell County came under military authority, Latter-day Saints living in Daviess County were forced to temporarily move to Far West, and sixty-four Mormon men were arrested—eleven of whom, including Joseph Smith, were incarcerated in Missouri prisons. During the winter and early spring of 1839, six to seven thousand Mormons made their way out of the state.

The events of the Mormon-Missouri War set the stage for a discussion of the most tragic episode of the regional conflict—the assault and massacre against the Mormons at Hawn's Mill in eastern Caldwell County on October 30, 1838.

NOTES

1. Joseph Smith Jr. to Emma Smith, April 4, 1839, Beinecke Rare Book and Manuscript Library, Yale University, New Haven, Connecticut; spelling standardized.

2. Lilburn W. Boggs to John B. Clark, October 27, 1838, *Mormon War Papers, 1837–1841*, Office of Secretary of State, Record Group 5, Missouri State Archives, Jefferson City, Missouri (hereafter cited as *MWP*); also in *Document Containing the Correspondence, Orders, &C. In Relation to the Disturbances with the Mormons; And the Evidence Given Before the Hon. Austin A. King, Judge of the Fifth Judicial Circuit of the State of Missouri, at the Court-House in Richmond, in a Criminal Court of Inquiry, Begun November 12, 1838, on the Trial of Joseph Smith, Jr., and Others, for High Treason and Other Crimes Against the State* (Fayette, MO: Boon's Lick Democrat, 1841), 61 (hereafter cited as *Document*).

3. W. W. Phelps to Church leaders in Kirtland, *Latter Day Saints' Messenger and Advocate* 3, no. 10 (July 1837):529.

4. Adam Black, statement, July 28, 1838, National Archives, Washington, DC.

5. Dean C. Jessee, Mark Ashurst-McGee, and Richard L. Jensen, eds., *Journals, Volume 1: 1832–1839*, vol. 1 of the Journal series of *The Joseph Smith Papers*, ed. Dean C. Jessee, Ronald K. Esplin, and Richard Lyman Bushman (Salt Lake City: Church Historian's Press, 2008), 242 (hereafter cited as *JSP*, J1). Joseph Smith responded to Boynton's belief in a divine guarantee by telling him that "if this had been declared, no one had authority from him for so doing, for he had always said unless the institution was conducted on righteous principles it would not stand." Ibid., 242–243, spelling standardized.

6. Phoebe Woodruff to Wilford Woodruff, March 1, 1838, Wilford Woodruff Collection, Church History Library, Salt Lake City, Utah (hereafter cited as CHL); spelling standardized.

7. Minute Book 2, 104–108, CHL; spelling standardized.

8. *JSP*, J1:244; spelling standardized.

9. Oliver Cowdery to Warren Cowdery, January 21, 1838, Oliver Cowdery Letter Book, 1833–1838, copy, MS 12174, CHL.

10. See *JSP*, J1:251–256.

11. John Corrill, *A Brief History of the Church of Christ of Latter Day Saints, (Commonly Called Mormons;) including an Account of Their Doctrine and Discipline; with the Reasons of the Author for Leaving the Church* (St. Louis, Printed for the Author: 1839), 30; also in Karen Lynn Davidson, Richard L. Jensen, and David J. Whitaker, eds., *Histories 2, Assigned Histories, 1831–1847*, vol. 2 of the Histories series of *The Joseph Smith Papers*, ed., Dean C. Jessee, Ronald K. Esplin, and Richard Lyman Bushman (Salt Lake City: The Church Historians Press, 2012), 165 (hereafter cited as *JSP*, H2).

12. *JSP*, J1:293; spelling standardized.

13. Sampson Avard and others to Oliver Cowdery, David Whitmer, John Whitmer, William W. Phelps, and Lyman E. Johnson, June 1838, in *Document*, 103.

14. *JSP*, J1:278.

15. *JSP*, J1:284.

16. Vinson Knight to William Cooper, February 1839, CHL. Reed Peck, following his excommunication, also wrote that the immigration to Daviess County "made the Mormons there equal in strength with the former citizens." Reed Peck, "Sketch of Mormon History," 1839, 20, mssHM 54459, Huntington Library, Huntington, California.

17. David Thomas to Joseph Smith, March 31, 1838, copy, *JSP*, J1:248.

18. John Murdock, Journal, John Murdock Papers, fd 2, 95, CHL; spelling standardized.

19. Joseph Smith, Sidney Rigdon, and others To the Publick [*sic*], n. d., Joseph Smith Collection, CHL.

20. Murdock, Journal, fd 2, 95; spelling standardized.

21. "Missouri Election," *Daily Commercial Bulletin*, August 21, 1838. It is significant to note that on May 5, 1838, John Wilson, a Whig candidate for a seat in the U.S. House of Representatives, visited Far West to campaign, hoping to recapture the formerly Whig House seat that had been lost to the Democratic party in 1836. However, Wilson's hopes of persuading the Mormons to align with the Whig party were quickly dashed. On May 10, Sidney Rigdon delivered a public address to "a large concourse of People from all quarters of the county and even from other counties . . . in consequence of One Gen. Wilsons speech." George W. Robinson observed: "The Politics of this Church (with but few exceptions only,) are that of the Democracy; which is also the feelings of the speaker who spoke this day, and all of the First Presidency." See *JSP*, J1:266–268; spelling standardized. Regardless, Wilson's visit illustrates the realization by many of the Missourians that the Mormons were experiencing an expanding political base.

22. Joseph Smith, Sidney Rigdon and others To the Publick [*sic*], n. d.

23. Vinson Knight to William Cooper, February 3, 1839.

24. Corrill, *A Brief History of the Church of Christ of Latter Day Saints*, 33; also in *JSP*, H2:170.

25. See William G. Hartley, *My Best for the Kingdom: History and Autobiography of John Lowe Butler, a Mormon Frontiersman* (Salt Lake City: Aspen Books, 1993), 51–61.

26. *JSP*, J1:298–299; spelling standardized.

27. *JSP*, J1:290–291.

28. Joseph Smith Jr., affidavit, September 5, 1838, MS 155, bx 4, fd 1, Joseph Smith Collection, CHL; spelling standardized.

29. Smith, affidavit, September 5, 1838.

30. Adam Black, affidavit, August 28, 1838, *MWP*; also in *Document*, 15.

31. Smith, affidavit, September 5, 1838.

32. Adam Black, statement, July 28, 1838, National Archives, Washington, DC.

33. *JSP*, J1:301. Significantly, John Williams may have been doing some double-dealing. After meeting with the Mormons, he certified an affidavit to Adam Black that the "Mormon encampment" at Black's house consisted of five hundred Mormon men, an inflated number that Williams had to have known was going to be used by Black to arouse public resistance in neighboring Ray County. See "Mormon War," *Daily Missouri Republican,* September 3, 1838.

34. *JSP*, J1:301.

35. "To the Citizens of Carroll County," *The Missourian*, September 1, 1838.

36. Daniel Ashby, James Keyte, and Sterling Price to Lilburn W. Boggs, September 1, 1838, *MWP*; also in *Document*, 15–16.

37. Joseph Dickson to Lilburn W. Boggs, September 6, 1838, *MWP*; also in *Document*, 17.

38. B. M. Lisle to David R. Atchison, August 30, 1838, *MWP*; also in *Document*, 20.

39. *JSP*, J1:318; spelling standardized.

40. Vinson Knight to William Cooper, February 3, 1839.

41. "The Mormons," *Daily Commercial Bulletin*, September 22, 1838, reprinted from the *Western Star*, September 14, 1838.

42. Alexander W. Doniphan to David R. Atchison, September 15, 1838, *MWP*; also in *Document*, 24–25.

43. See Hiram G. Parks to Lilburn W. Boggs, September 25, 1838, *MWP*; also in *Document*, 32–33.

44. Mormon petitioners in DeWitt, Carroll County, to Lilburn W. Boggs, September 22, 1838, *MWP*, also in *Document*, 29–30; spelling standardized.

45. John W. Price and William K. Logan, Report of the Committee of Chariton County, October 5, 1838, *MWP*; also in *Documen*t, 36.

46. Hiram G. Parks to David R. Atchison, October 7, 1838, *MWP*, October 1838; also in *Document*, 37–38; spelling standardized.

47. David R. Atchison to Lilburn W. Boggs, October 9, 1838, *MWP*; also in *Document*, 38.

48. Corrill, *A Brief History of the Church of Christ of Latter Day Saints*, 36; also in *JSP*, H2:175.

49. "Extract, from the Private Journal of Joseph Smith Jr.," *Times and Seasons* 1, no. 1 (November 1839):3.

50. "Extract, from the Private Journal of Joseph Smith Jr.," 4.

51. "The Mormons," *Daily Commercial Bulletin*, September 27, 1838, reprinted from the *Columbia Patriot*.

52. "The Mormon War," *Daily Herald and Gazette,* October 13, 1838, reprinted from the *St. Louis Republican*.

53. David R. Atchison to Lilburn W. Boggs, October 16, 1838, *MWP*; also in *Document*, 39.

54. Corrill, *A Brief History of the Church of Christ of Latter Day Saints*, 36; also in *JSP*, H2:175–176; spelling standardized.

55. Corrill, *A Brief History of the Church of Christ of Latter Day Saints*, 36; also in *JSP*, H2:176.

56. William P. Peniston to Lilburn W. Boggs, October 21, 1838, *MWP*; also in *Document*, 43–44.

57. David R. Atchison to Lilburn W. Boggs, October 22, 1838, *MWP*; also in *Document*, 46–47.

58. Thomas B. Marsh, affidavit, October 24, 1838, in *Document*, 57–59.

59. Orson Hyde, affidavit, October 24, 1838, in *Document*, 59.

60. Citizens of Ray County to Lilburn W. Boggs, October 23, 1838, *MWP*; also in *Document*, 49.

61. B. M. Lisle to John B. Clark, October 26, 1838, *MWP*; also in *Document*, 62–63.

62. Samuel Bogart to General David R. Atchison, October 23, 1838, *MWP*; also in *Document*, 48. Atchison subsequently authorized Bogart to conduct the patrol. See David R. Atchison to Samuel Bogart, October 23, 1838, *MWP*; also in *Document*, 108.

63. A descriptive account of the battle is found in Alexander L. Baugh, *A Call to Arms: The 1838 Mormon Defense of Northern Missouri* (Provo, UT: Joseph Fielding Smith Institute for Latter-day Saint History and BYU Studies, 2000), 99–113. See also Erin B. Metcalfe, "'Firm and Steadfast in the Faith': Patterson O'Banion and the Battle of Crooked River," *Mormon Historical Studies* 14, no. 2 (Fall 2013): 109–121.

64. Sarshel Woods and Joseph Dickson, letter of October 24, 1838, MWP; also in *Document*, 60. The letter should be dated October 25, 1838.

65. Wiley Williams and Amos Rees to John B. Clark, October 25, 1838, *MWP*; also in *Document*, 60.

66. Lilburn W. Boggs to John B. Clark, October 27, 1838, *MWP*; also in *Document*, 61.

3

Jacob Hawn and the Hawn's Mill Settlement in Eastern Caldwell County

Alexander L. Baugh

Jacob Hawn, the original founder of the Hawn's Mill settlement, was one of four children born to Henry Hawn, who was born in Germany. As a young man, Henry immigrated to Canada, relocated in Pennsylvania, and finally settled in Genesee County, New York. Henry and his wife had four children—Jacob, James, Michael, and Mary.

Jacob was born January 13, 1804, in Genesee County. As a young man, Jacob married a woman by the last name of Myers who died early in their marriage before bearing any children. On November 18, 1833, Jacob, then twenty-eight, married his second wife, fifteen-year-old Harriett Elizabeth Pierson (also recorded as Pearson), a marriage that is reported to have taken place near Buffalo, New York. Harriett was born on August 31, 1818, in Newark, Hudson County, New Jersey. She lost her parents at a young age and was raised by extended family members who lived in Cattaraugus County. Shortly after their marriage, Jacob and Harriett left New York and moved to an area near Green Bay, Wisconsin, where he built at least one mill and possibly more.[1] Here, their first daughter, Laura, was born on September 1, 1835.[2]

Sometime in late 1835, the Hawn family moved to western Missouri. Land records show that on December 7, 1835, Jacob entered a claim for forty acres on Shoal Creek in what was at that time a sparsely settled part of Ray County, making the Hawns among some of the earliest settlers in that part of the county.[3] Significantly, Hawn's 1835 land record shows the spelling as being *H-a-w-n*, not *H-a-u-n*.[4] Early Mormon sources and narratives give both spellings (though *H-a-u-n* is still the more common), but references made to Jacob and Harriett in histories of Oregon—where they emigrated in 1843 and where they both died—and virtually every family source always use *H-a-w-n*. Even their grave markers use the "w" spelling—a clear

In 1835, Jacob Hawn, the son of German immigrants, settled his family on virgin land in northern Missouri, where he built a mill.

Two misconceptions have been perpetuated in history. The first is that Jacob and Harriet Hawn were Mormons; they were not. The second is the spelling of their name. It is not spelled *H-a-u-n*, but rather *H-a-w-n*.

indication of the correct spelling. Missouri state histories, county histories, and Missouri atlases generally use *H-a-u-n*, which probably explains why most historical literature written about the massacre uses that spelling. Furthermore, given the structure of the name and its phonetics, it is easy to see how the *u* spelling was adopted. But if we are to be historically accurate, *H-a-w-n* is the correct spelling.[5]

It appears that Jacob and Harriett Hawn had not been affiliated with Mormonism before coming to Missouri in late 1835, and, in fact, they were never Mormons. Historians who have written about the Mormon–Missouri period have simply assumed they were Mormons, mainly because they settled in what became a Mormon county and lived among members of the Church. This is not to say that before coming to Missouri the Hawns were unaware of the Church or had never heard of Joseph Smith and the Book of Mormon. The fact that Jacob was born and raised in Genesee County, New York—situated fewer than fifty miles from Wayne and Ontario counties—and resided in western New York until late 1833 suggests that he and Harriett had probably heard some reports concerning the "Mormonites." En route to Wisconsin from New York, they may have passed through northeastern Ohio, perhaps even Kirtland, where they could have come across or heard about the Mormons.

One of the strongest arguments supporting the conclusion that Jacob and Harriett Hawn were not Mormons is the fact that none of the Latter-day Saints who actually lived at or in the vicinity of Hawn's Mill (and therefore those who personally knew the Hawns) ever mentions in a narrative anything about the Hawns in connection with membership in the Church. Simply stated, Jacob and Harriett were an adventuresome couple who thrived on the prospects and opportunities of the American frontier—first in the remote northern region of Wisconsin, then in northwestern Missouri, and finally in the Willamette Valley of Oregon Territory, where they relocated in 1843. They simply bumped into Mormonism in Missouri in the mid–1830s, left Missouri in late 1838 or early 1839, and made their own way to the West in the early 1840s.[6]

This photo gives some idea of what the forty acres Hawn purchased on Shoal Creek may have looked like. Hawn's Mill would find itself just sixteen miles east of Far West, the largest Mormon settlement in the area.

After he purchased his forty-acre property in December 1835, it probably took Jacob Hawn several months to build his mill and begin operations. As an experienced miller, he no doubt recognized the agricultural and economic potential of the region and believed that the area's surrounding population, at that time and in the future, would support the enterprise. He did not have to wait long for additional neighbors. As part of the relocation agreement made from May to August 1836 between the Mormons and Clay County leaders and citizens, Mormon leaders began searching out and purchasing land parcels near Shoal Creek, approximately sixteen miles to the west of Hawn's property. Part of that property purchase became Far West, the new Mormon center.

CREATION OF CALDWELL COUNTY FOR THE MORMONS

During the fall 1836 Missouri legislative session, Alexander W. Doniphan, Clay County's representative to the state legislature and the Mormons' hired attorney, introduced legislation proposing the creation of a county for the Mormons situated north of what was considered "incorporated" Ray County. Doniphan initially proposed the county be twenty-four miles square. However, a number of non-Mormons living between the fifty-third and fifty-fourth township lines protested being included in the Mormon county, so a region six by twenty-four square miles called the Buncombe Strip was attached to Ray County, leaving the proposed Mormon county eighteen by twenty-four square miles. As discussions progressed, Doniphan began to fear that the bill to organize one county exclusively for the Mormons might not pass,

Alexander W. Doniphan—attorney, soldier, and politician—was serving in the Missouri State Legislature in 1836. He was instrumental in the creation of Caldwell County as a place for the Latter-day Saints. For this and other efforts on behalf of the Mormons, Doniphan was given a hero's welcome when he visited Salt Lake City in 1878.

so he proposed that a second county (essentially a non-Mormon county) also be created directly north of the proposed Mormon county. The bill passed the House on December 23 and the Senate on December 27. On December 29, Governor Lilburn W. Boggs signed legislation that created Caldwell County (situated directly north of Ray County) in behalf of the Mormons, and Daviess County, essentially for non-Mormons, directly north of Caldwell.[7]

With the creation of Caldwell County, Hawn's property and the settlement community became part of the Mormon county. It was later reported that "every Gentile in the proposed new county that could be induced to sell his possessions at a reasonable price was bought out, and his place taken by a Mormon."[8] Hawn, however, would have been an exception. His decision to stay and not sell out probably stemmed from several factors. He had clearly made a substantial investment in his milling operation. Whereas a typical farmer could simply sell his land and cabin and start over, a milling operation represented a sizeable building project. After all, the construction of a dam, a millrace, and the mill itself, including the mechanical gear, represented a significant investment in equipment and construction—something most mill owners were not likely to just walk away from. Hawn also probably enjoyed brisk business and apparently did not have any objections to the Mormon people, but in fact saw them as business patrons and customers.[9]

MORMON SETTLEMENT IN THE VICINITY OF HAWN'S MILL

Significantly, Jacob Hawn was joined by a few other enterprising Mormon millers. The first of these, Robert White, purchased one hundred and sixty acres of land on August 2, 1836, eighty acres of which was located about a half mile northeast and downstream from Hawn's property, where White established a second mill.[10] In July 1837, Jacob Myers Jr. purchased a forty-acre plot immediately west and upstream from Hawn. Here, Myers and his father, Jacob Sr., built

a rudimentary saw mill.[11] Still later, the Myerses partnered with Ellis Eames and added a gristmill operation to the saw mill.[12] With three milling operations in the immediate area, Mormons often referred to the general locality of Hawn's Mill simply as "the mills."

The presence of three mills also suggests there was plenty of business to go around, and each of the enterprises likely turned a handsome profit. Hawn's success may have led him to encourage his brother, James Hawn, to move to Caldwell County. In November 1837, James Hawn purchased forty acres directly southwest of Jacob Hawn's forty-acre property.[13] Little is known about James Hawn, but whereas no record exists to show that Jacob became a Mormon, apparently James did. James McBride, a Latter-day Saint, later wrote that in June 1838 he, Isaac Leany, and James Hawn were all baptized into the Church at the same time.[14]

The actual settlement of Hawn's Mill never included more than a few families and fewer than a dozen cabins. However, another seventy to seventy-five Latter-day Saint families lived in the immediate area, mostly in Fairview Township along Shoal Creek.[15] These Saints and a number of local Gentile settlers in the region, including a number living in nearby Livingston County, came from several miles around to get their milling done by the enterprising mill owners. In addition to operating as an important agricultural production center for the region, the settlement also served as a stopping place for Mormons coming from

With the influx of Mormons into the area, business was brisk and other mills would be constructed, bringing the total to three on Shoal Creek.

Hawn's Mill Settlement by Nancy Harlacher of the Community of Christ Church.

the East en route to Far West. When a branch of the Church was also later established, David Evans was called to preside over the members.[16] Accepting the conclusion that Jacob Hawn was not a Latter-day Saint helps us understand why Evans, not Hawn, was appointed branch president.

PRELUDE TO THE ATTACK

It was here on this site at Crooked River, Missouri, that a battle was fought between Mormon and Missouri militia forces. It was in part because of the aggressive actions of the Mormons here at Crooked River that the vigilantes of Livingston County justified their attack on Hawn's Mill.

The Mormon "cleansing" of Daviess County during the latter part of October, coupled with the erroneous reports that Bogart's forces had been routed and then annihilated at Crooked River on October 24–25, sent a signal to vigilante groups in northern Missouri that more extreme measures would have to be undertaken in order to restore local control and bring about complete Mormon submission. Anti-Mormon forces, principally from Livingston County, assisted by a number of Daviess refugees and a handful of community regulators from other locales, were the first to respond to the Mormon strikes and did so in a retaliatory fashion. In writing about the Missourians who carried out the tragedy at Hawn's Mill, nineteenth-century Missouri historian Return I. Holcombe wrote:

> Nearly all of the men were citizens of Livingston County. Perhaps twenty were from Daviess, from whence they had been driven by the Mormons during the troubles in that county a few weeks previously. The Daviess County men were very bitter against the Mormons, and vowed the direst vengeance on the entire sect. It did not matter whether or not the Mormons at the mill had taken any part in the disturbance which had occurred [in Daviess]; it was enough that they were Mormons. The Livingston men became thoroughly imbued with the same spirit, and all were eager for the raid, . . . feel[ing] an extraordinary sympathy for the outrages suffered by their neighbors.[17]

The historical sources demonstrate that the main objective of the Livingston and Daviess marauders was to make the Mormons *pay* for their most recent activities conducted against the non-Mormon settlers in Daviess and at Crooked River. And the Mormons at Hawn's Mill became the target.

Crooked Creek, photo by Brent Lyman.

The Mormons living at the mill and along Shoal Creek were on relatively friendly terms with their non-Mormon neighbors until the problems erupted in Daviess County in mid-October. "All things continued to move on well; the inhabitants behaved themselves very friendly and purchased goods from [us] and used my mill for grinding and sawing," recalled Ellis Eames. "This continued until the disturbances broke out up in Daviess county, when I observed from the conversation that they did not like the proceedings of our brethren."[18] Fearful they might expect treatment similar to that received by their neighbors to the north, Gentile settlers living in eastern Caldwell sought help from Livingston's vigilante forces, whose numbers were now strengthened by embittered Daviess County refugees recently displaced from their homes. Two non-Mormons, Sardius Smith and George Miller, who lived in the vicinity of Hawn's Mill, were not only afraid of possible Mormon harassment, but feared they might be mistaken as Latter-day Saints and thus mobbed by vigilante forces. To avoid any maltreatment altogether, Smith and Miller abandoned most of their property in the latter part of October, moved to Livingston County, and then hired a band of locals to go to Caldwell County and bring back their belongings.[19]

The antagonism against the Hawn's Mill community was also fueled by Latter-day Saint dissidents who left the religious society and then spread false and misleading reports concerning Mormon intentions. One such individual may have been Robert White. As noted, White was one of the first Mormons to settle in the area of Shoal Creek in 1834. However, by late October 1838, he became disillusioned with the Church, abandoned his mill, and moved to Livingston County.[20] Significantly, several Mormon sources report White as being a member of the Livingston force that attacked the mill.[21]

Following the Mormon War, Daniel Ashby—a resident of Brunswick, Chariton County; a member of the Missouri State Senate; and a Hawn's Mill massacre participant—testified before the state senate that the reports given by Mormon dissenters who had moved into his county were the primary reason for the decision to attack the mill. "They [the dissenters] reported that the Mormons intended attacking the people on our line, and that they intended burning a town." Ashby said further

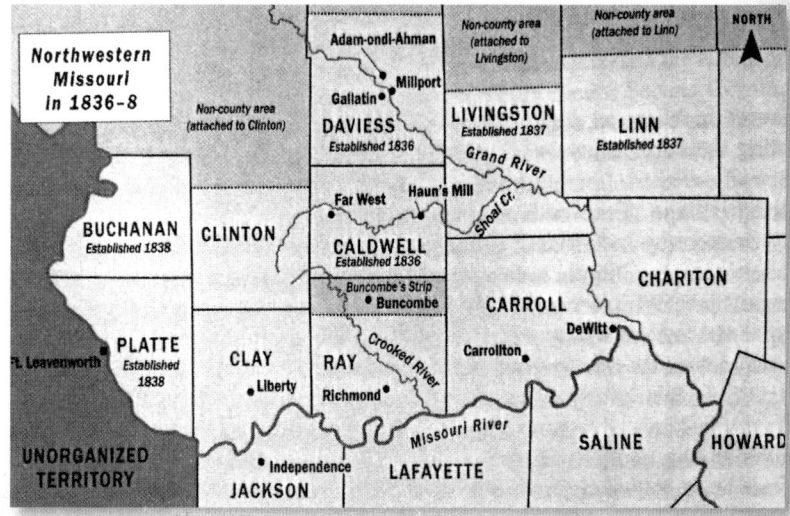

The Latter-day Saints living along Shoal Creek enjoyed peaceful relations with their neighbors until violence broke out in Daviess County to the west. Those non-Mormons driven out of Daviess County fled to Livingston County for refuge. There they joined with others in a vigilante force bent on revenge against the Mormons. The closest target upon which to vent their wrath was the settlement at Hawn's Mill.

Missouri County Map by John Hamer.

that out of fear the Mormons would attack, "we thought it best to attack them first. . . . What we did was in our own defense, and as we had the right to do."²²

HARASSMENT OF MORMON COMPANIES AND SETTLERS

Livingston's community regulators were quick to respond to the rumors. "The people living on Grand River about 6 or 8 miles north of the mill began to come over to Shoal Creek settlements where the Mormons lived and drove off our cattle and made some threats that they intended to come and burn down the mills," wrote David Lewis.²³ Since the mills were the economic and temporal lifeblood of the entire Mormon population in the region, the decision was made to post a continual guard to prevent any attempts to burn the structures.²⁴

However, the threats soon escalated even further. Around October 25, a band of approximately twenty men, headed up by Nehemiah Comstock of Livingston County, rode into Hawn's Mill, demanding that the Mormons turn over their guns and weapons. Fearing negative repercussions if the ruffians' directives were not met, most of the men reluctantly complied. Hiram Abbot, however, refused, knowing the men had no authority to issue such orders. Fearing immediate retribution at the hands of the company members, Abbot ran, making his way across the mill dam and up the hill on the other side. Comstock and two other vigilante members, Elijah Trosper and Joshua Whitney, quickly dismounted and went in pursuit. While Abbot was in the act of climbing the hill on the opposite bank, Comstock took aim, making several attempts to shoot, but the cartridge misfired each time. Seeing his attacker's dilemma, Abbot turned his gun on Comstock, who sought cover behind a hen house. This gave Abbot the break he needed to make his escape, and he darted away. Realizing a chase would prove useless, Comstock called Whitney and Trosper off, and the company left, satisfied that they were able to confiscate nearly all the weapons in the community. As soon as the anti-Mormon band made their departure, messengers were dispatched to send word to Mormon families living along Shoal Creek that hostile bands were active in the area and to be on guard.²⁵

Anti-Mormon raiders also accosted Mormon companies traveling through the area en route to Far West. Abraham Palmer reported that while passing through Livingston County, his company was surrounded by a mob consisting of thirty-eight

Joseph Young, the brother of Brigham Young, was leading a company of Latter-day Saints from Kirtland to Far West. As they were passing through Livingston County, they were detained and all their weapons were confiscated. Young's company sought refuge at Hawn's Mill.

Joseph Young, courtesy of the Church Archives, The Church of Jesus Christ of Latter-day Saints.

men who abused them and then took the only three rifles they had before allowing them to pass on.[26] William H. Walker's wagon company was stopped in the same area. Every wagon was searched and robbed of all its firearms and ammunitions, and the drivers were warned that if they proceeded any farther, they would all be killed. Two Mormon men were also taken prisoner.[27] Captain William Mann and his group of Livingston guards were the likely culprits in these two detainments.[28]

Another Mormon company led by Joseph Young, brother of Brigham Young, received even harsher treatment. While passing through Livingston County, Young's party, composed of some ten families, was confronted by a Livingston band headed by County Clerk Thomas R. Bryan, his brother Jefferson Bryan, William Ewell, and James Austin. "We were taken prisoners by an armed mob that . . . demanded every bit of ammunition and every weapon we had," wrote Amanda Smith. "We surrendered all. They knew it, for they searched our wagons."[29] The raiders then took them back a distance of five miles to a location known as Whitney's Mills, where they were placed under guard and detained for three days. After finally being released, Young's company proceeded on to Hawn's Mill, where they arrived two days before the attack.[30]

After confiscating what weapons they could from both Mormon settlers and emigrants, vigilante leaders next sent messengers to the Mormon community, proposing that the two sides meet together to bring about terms of reconciliation. "The mob . . . sent word to us that they wished to meet a committee of our people and have an understanding of each other's movements and expressed their wish to live in peace and friendly terms with us," wrote Ellis Eames.[31] The Mormons were more than willing to oblige, recognizing that they were at a distinct disadvantage, having only a limited number of weapons as well as being outnumbered by the addition of vigilantes from Livingston, Daviess, and other surrounding counties. Accordingly, David Evans, Jacob Myers Sr., and Anthony Blackburn were selected to represent the Mormons in the discussions.

The mills' leaders negotiated with leaders of several vigilante groups on different occasions. One meeting was held at the Myers settlement, situated a few miles east of Hawn's Mill. Here, the three Mormon delegates arbitrated with Samuel E. Todd, Zachariah Lee, Isaac McCroskie, Thomas R. Bryan, and William F. Ewell, all from Livingston County.[32] About this same time, President Evans deliberated a truce by means of a messenger with Nehemiah Comstock, at which time both parties agreed to abandon their military organizations.[33] In addition, at least

David Evans served as the branch president at Hawn's Mill and was also appointed to negotiate peace with the mob forces in the area. Just days before the attack, the vigilantes agreed to a truce. David Evans was among those who survived the subsequent attack.

David Evans, courtesy of the Church History Library.

While the mob ostensibly negotiated terms of peace, the historical evidence indicates that it was a ploy to disarm the Mormons and give the vigilantes the advantage during the actual attack.

Opposite Top: Jacob Hawn came to Far West to counsel with the Prophet Joseph Smith regarding whether the Saints at Hawn's Mill should remain at the mill or move to Far West for safety. Joseph's counsel was decidedly to move out of the mill settlement. Hawn never delivered the Prophet's counsel to the Saints at Hawn's Mill.

two meetings were held at the home of Oliver Walker, attended by local citizens representing the non-Mormon settlers living among the Mormons in Fairview Township in Caldwell County. A third meeting was probably held with the members of this same group on the day of the attack.[34] In each of these exchanges, both sides agreed to leave the other alone and live peaceably.

Historical evidence, however, suggests that the attempts made by the vigilantes to confiscate the Mormons' weapons, followed by the peace negotiations, were actually part of the overall plan of the Missouri regulators to ensure the eradication of the Mormon community. By disarming the Latter-day Saints—both those living in the area as well as those traveling through the region—the mobs left the Mormons defenseless, making it possible for the attack on the community to take place with minimal resistance and reducing the risk of casualties. The pretended truce was conducted so that the Mormons would be led to believe they had nothing to fear and that an attack was not likely to occur.[35] The Mormons, however, were neither totally naive nor unsuspecting of their enemies' possible intentions. At the conclusion of these negotiations, Ellis Eames wrote: "We felt more satisfied, having, as we thought, a perfect understanding of their intentions, but at the same time we thought it best to keep up a watch at the mills for fear any individuals might come privately and burn them."[36] A few Mormon families living in the surrounding area moved to the mills and boarded with other Mormon families. "We gathered to Hawn's

Staging the Attack © Kelly Donovan.

Mill for the double purpose of our better security," David Fullmer remembered, "and saving the mill from being burned."[37]

COUNSEL TO MOVE TO FAR WEST

Fearing the possibility of some sort of confrontation, residents of the mill community appointed Jacob Hawn to travel to Far West to seek advice from Caldwell County militia leaders and Mormon leaders concerning whether they should continue to maintain the mill site and remain in the area. The meeting reportedly took place on October 25, five days before the massacre.[38] While at Far West, Hawn first approached John Killian, an officer in the Caldwell militia. Recognizing the isolated nature of the settlement and its proximity to the hostile Livingston and Carroll county forces, Killian counseled Hawn to move the families to Far West at once.[39] The mill owner also asked Joseph Smith for his counsel concerning the situation, whereupon he was told to abandon the mill so as to not risk the lives of the citizens. "But we think we are strong enough to defend the mill and keep it in our own hands," Hawn is reported to have replied. With that, he returned to the community and reported falsely that Joseph Smith's instructions were for them to stay and protect and hold the mill.[40]

David Lewis believed Hawn purposely misrepresented the Prophet's position and deliberately deceived community members. He wrote that Hawn "returned and said if we thought we could maintain the mill it was Joseph's [counsel] for us to do so . . . and not to come to Far West and we thought from the way the thing was represented it would be like cowards to leave and not try to maintain it . . . [and] we thought to gather up all our affects and leave our houses would be useless, for we did not know that it was Joseph's decided [counsel] for us to do so."[41] Lewis's statement is supported by Philo Dibble, who, although not a Hawn's Mill resident, reported to have knowledge concerning the conversation between Hawn and Joseph Smith. "While I was at Far West," he wrote, "Brother Joseph had sent word by Hawn, who owned the mill, to inform the brethren who were living there to leave and come to Far West, but Mr. Hawn did not deliver the message."[42]

Philo Dibble was a witness to the conversation between Joseph Smith and Jacob Hawn. Dibble further attested to the fact that Hawn did not accurately deliver the Prophet's message.

Concerning the instruction and counsel Hawn received from the Prophet to abandon the mill and settlement and move into Far West, John D. Lee wrote in his memoir: "The massacre at Hawn's Mill was the result of the brethren's refusal to obey the wishes of the Prophet. All the brethren so considered it. It made a deep and lasting impression on my mind, for I had heard the Prophet give the counsel . . . to come into the town [Far West]. They had refused, and the result was a lesson to all that there was no safety except in obeying the Prophet."[43] Joseph Smith's manuscript history states that several years later in Nauvoo, the Prophet was reported to have said: "None had ever been killed who abode by my counsel. At Hawn's Mill the brethren went contrary to my counsel; if they had not, their lives would have been spared."[44] Ultimately, however, the Hawn's Mill Saints themselves should not bear the blame for rejecting Joseph Smith's instruction and counsel. Had Hawn reported the Prophet's counsel truthfully, presumably most of the community members would have followed the Mormon leader's recommendation and moved into Far West. Thus, if responsibility is to be affixed to anyone, that individual must be Jacob Hawn, not the members of the community at large.

Around noon on Sunday, October 28, Joseph Young's emigrant company arrived at Hawn's Mill, "where we found a number of our friends, collected together who were holding a council; and deliberating on the best course for them to pursue," Young wrote.[45] By this time, Jacob Hawn had returned from his meeting with Mormon leaders in Far West, and the community was likely meeting in order to hear his report and discuss their situation. At the same time, community leaders were also aware that William Mann and his band had been harassing Mormon emigrants. With the recent arrival of Young and his group, and learning from them that they had been detained for three days by Bryan and his Livingston men, it became even clearer that their antagonists had no intentions of keeping their agreements.

The community faced only two options—they could abandon their homes and move into Far West, or they could remain and try to protect themselves and

Below: Just before the attack, members of Joseph Young's Kirtland Camp arrived at Hawn's Mill and were living in tents around the blacksmith shop.

Blacksmith Shop © Kirt Harmon; for more information, visit www.harmonartonline.com.

their property. Jacob Myers Sr. favored leaving, reminding the group how few they were in comparison with the number on the side of the "Gentiles."[46] However, Hawn's "twisted" report tended to encourage them to remain, and "the decision of council," wrote Joseph Young, "was that our friends there should place themselves in an attitude of self-defense . . . [and be] in constant readiness for an attack of any small body of men that might come upon them."[47] Young's company was also compelled to remain at the mills for another reason. For a number of days they had been short on rations. After arriving at the Mormon settlement they purchased what grain they needed and then concluded to remain until it could be ground.[48] The families camped in tents in the center of the community near the blacksmith shop owned by James Houston.[49] With the addition of Young's group (approximately ten families), the total number of Mormon families living at or near the mills came to about thirty. Thirty-five to forty adult men were on hand to defend the community.[50]

The community prepared a hasty defense. Although many of their firearms had already been seized as a result of the raids conducted by Comstock's men, they set to work collecting what weapons could be found, including squirrel rifles and shotguns, while the women offered to mold bullets and prepare powder patches.[51] Community leaders also

The Saints at Hawn's Mill suspected an attack and planned accordingly. The blacksmith shop was the place appointed as a defense garrison in the event of attack, and it was there the Saints staged their remaining weapons and posted guards.

made guard assignments and established night watches. Finally, the blacksmith shop was set up to be a garrison or block-house should an assault on the community take place.[52] They did not have to wait long.

NOTES

1. The main published biographical sources for information on the early years of Jacob and Harriett Hawn comes from *History of the Willamette Valley Oregon*, vol. 3 (Chicago, IL: S. J. Clarke Publishing Company, 1927), 634; and *The Centennial History of Oregon, 1811–1912*, vol. 2 (Chicago, IL: S. J. Clark Publishing Company, 1912), 1036. Both volumes include information about the Hawns under the biographical sketch of W. R. Bunn, son of John M. and Mary E. Hawn Bunn. Mary was a daughter of Jacob and Harriett Hawn, making W. R. a grandson. Other sources containing biographical information include *Pioneer Families of Yamhill County, Oregon*, vol. 2 (Lafayette, OR: n. p., 1953), 300; and Shirley H. O'Neil, *Yamhill County Pioneers*, vol. 1 (n. p., 2004), 275–280.

2. Laura gives her own birth date in Laura Aurvilla Hawn Perkins Patterson, "Recollections," typescript, 1, Yamhill County Historical Society, Lafayette, Oregon; copy in possession of the author. Another Hawn family history was prepared by Leviaette (Levia) S. Hawn Patterson, also a daughter of Jacob and Harriett Hawn. See Leviaette (Levia) S. Hawn Patterson, "History," typescript, Yamhill County Historical Society, Lafayette, Oregon, copy in possession of the author.

3. See Record #252, Original Entries for Lands in Caldwell County, Caldwell County Records Office, Kingston, Missouri, NW ¼ of NE ¼ of Section 17; also Clark V. Johnson and Ronald E. Romig, with revisions by Annette W. Curtis, *An Index to Early Caldwell County, Missouri Land Records* (Independence, MO: Missouri Mormon Frontier Foundation, 2005), 81; and Jeffrey N. Walker, "Mormon Land Rights in Caldwell and Daviess Counties and the Mormon Conflict of 1838," *BYU Studies* 47, no. 1 (2008):25, n57. The forty-acre property later became part of Fairview Township in Caldwell County. See John Hamer, *Northeast of Eden: A Historical Atlas of Missouri's Mormon County* (Independence, MO: John Whitmer Books, 2011), 54. The *History of Caldwell and Livingston Counties, Missouri*, has Jacob Hawn establishing his mill on Shoal Creek in 1834. See *History of Caldwell and Livingston Counties, Missouri* (St. Louis, MO: National Historical Company, 1886), 100. However, this could not be the case. As noted in the text, the Hawns' first daughter, Laura, was born in Wisconsin in September 1835, so they could not have been living in Missouri in 1834.

4. The name was probably anglicized by Henry Hawn, Jacob Hawn's father, from the German *H-a-h-n* to *H-a-w-n*.

5. It is significant to note that map illustrations in previous editions of the LDS Doctrine and Covenants used the *H-a-u-n* spelling to identify the settlement site. However, the map of Missouri on page 408 in the 2013 edition now gives the spelling as *H-a-w-n*.

6. For a detailed discussion of Jacob Hawn, the Hawn's Mill settlement, and his relocation to Oregon, see Alexander L. Baugh, "Jacob Hawn and the Hawn's Mill Massacre: Missouri Millwright and Oregon Pioneer," *Mormon Historical Studies* 11, no. 1 (Spring 2010):1–25.

7. See *History of Caldwell and Livingston Counties, Missouri*, 103–105; see also *Laws of the State of Missouri, 1st Session, 9th General Assembly, 1836–1837* (Jefferson City, MO: Jeffersonian Office, 1837), 46–47, 155, 188, 204.

8. *History of Caldwell and Livingston Counties*, 104. Although not every non-Mormon left, most probably did. Furthermore, it is safe to say that a few non-Mormons later moved in. Regardless, the county was clearly dominated by Mormons. "By the summer of 1838, the population of the county was about 5,000, of whom, it is safe to say, 4,900 were Mormons" (*History of Caldwell and Livingston Counties*, 118).

9. In November 1995, LaMar C. Berrett, professor of Church history and doctrine at BYU, assisted by Alexander L. Baugh, Charles Allen, John Eldridge, and Randy Olsen, with permission from the Reorganized Church of Jesus Christ of Latter Day Saints (now the Community of Christ), which owned the property, conducted an archaeological ground survey of Hawn's property. The team made two significant discoveries immediately southeast of the mill site on the south side of Shoal Creek. The first of these discoveries was the presence of an old wagon road leading directly to the mill and stream, likely used by people coming to the mill from the south. Even more significant was the discovery just a few feet from the road of a number of household items and artifacts, clearly suggesting the presence of a cabin. These discoveries are shown on the inset map in LaMar C. Berrett, *Sacred Places Volume Four: Missouri* (Salt Lake City: Deseret Book, 2004), 338; see also 347. Another study conducted by F. Richard Hauck of the Archaeological Research Institute in March 1999 used ground-penetrating radar to reveal the remains of a foundation or root cellar at the cabin location. These two discoveries led the team to conclude that this was the probable location of Hawn's cabin. This is further supported by the fact that historical sources indicate that Hawn's home was on the south side of Shoal Creek. He probably constructed his home at this location to be adjacent to or close by the mill. See F. Richard Hauck, "Historic Burials at Far West and Haun's [Hawn's] Mill: The Use of Ground-Penetrating Radar at Two Historic Mormon Sites in Northwestern Missouri," unpublished study, copy in the possession of the author. For a brief description of Hauck's study, see Alexander L. Baugh, "Mormon Historic Sites Foundation Sponsors Archaeological Research at Far West and Haun's [Hawn's] Mill," *Site & Scene* 2, no. 1 (Spring 2000):1–2. Hauck's study was funded by the Mormon Historic Sites Foundation.

10. The property purchased by Robert White for his mill consisted of eighty acres of the W½ of the SW¼ of Section 9. *Original Entries for Lands in Caldwell County*, Record #2590; see also Clark and Romig, *An Index to Early Caldwell County, Missouri Land Records*, 216. On this same date (August 2, 1836), White purchased two additional forty-acre tracts nearby, but not on Shoal Creek. See *Original Entries for Lands in Caldwell County*, Record #202 and #257; also Clark and Romig, *An Index to Early Caldwell County, Missouri Land Records*, 217. The *History of Caldwell and Livingston Counties* states that White purchased his mill property in 1834, but this is an error. See *History of Caldwell*

and Livingston Counties, 100, 476. White added two forty-acre parcels in 1837 and 1838. See *Original Entries for Lands in Caldwell County*, Record #208 and #249; also Clark and Romig, *An Index to Early Caldwell County, Missouri Land Records*, 217. By late October 1838, on becoming disillusioned with Mormonism, he moved to Livingston County. Ironically, a number of Mormons later wrote that he was a member of the vigilante party that attacked the mill.

11. The property purchased by Jacob Myers Jr. for his mill, transacted on July 29, 1837, consisted of forty acres of the NE¼ of the NW¼ of Section 17. *Original Entries for Lands in Caldwell County*, Record #251; see also Clark and Romig, *An Index to Early Caldwell County, Missouri Land Records*, 124. Both Jacob Myers Jr. and Jacob Myers Sr. purchased two hundred additional acres in the immediate area—a total of two hundred forty acres. See *Original Entries for Lands in Caldwell County*, Record #2595, #222, and #203; see also Clark and Romig, *An Index to Early Caldwell County, Missouri Land Records*, 124–125.

12. Ellis Eames, quoted in *Journal History of the Church*, October 30, 1838, 11, Church History Library, The Church of Jesus Christ of Latter-day Saints, Salt Lake City, Utah. Eames states that the modified mill was completed the following spring, namely 1838. He was somehow misidentified in the *Journal History* as Ellis Eamut and is sometimes also referred to as Ellis Ames.

13. The forty-acre property purchased by James Hawn included the SE¼ of the NE¼ of Section 17. *Original Entries for Lands in Caldwell County*, Record #248; also Clark and Romig, *An Index to Early Caldwell County, Missouri Land Records*, 81.

14. James McBride, "Autobiography of James McBride," typescript, 10, L. Tom Perry Special Collections, Harold B. Lee Library, Brigham Young University, Provo, Utah (hereafter cited as Perry, Special Collections).

15. Local history gives the names of some forty Mormons known to have made land entries in Fairview Township between 1835 and 1837. See *History of Caldwell and Livingston Counties*, 476–478.

16. McBride, "Autobiography," 10.

17. Return I. Holcombe [Burr Joyce], "The Haun's [Hawn's] Mill Massacre: An Incident of the 'Mormon War' in Missouri," in *St. Louis Globe-Democrat*, October 6, 1887, n. p.; also published in Joseph Smith III and Heman C. Smith, *The History of the Reorganized Church of Jesus Christ of Latter Day Saints*, 4 vols. (Independence: Herald House, 1951), 2:227. Holcombe, who wrote this narrative under the pen name of Burr Joyce, was a late nineteenth- and early twentieth-century historian who wrote several county and local histories of communities and locales in Kansas, Missouri, and Minnesota. Walter B. Stevens, a noted Missouri state historian, later stated that Holcombe was the most noted researcher and writer of the Mormon experience in Missouri. See Walter B. Stevens, *Centennial History of Missouri: One Hundred Years in the Union, 1820–1921*, 6 vols. (St. Louis: S. J. Clarke Publishing Company, 1921), 115–116.

18. Eames, quoted in *Journal History of the Church*, October 30, 1838, 11.

19. Eames, quoted in *Journal History of the Church*, October 30, 1838, 11. Isaac Leany, a Mormon who was wounded in the attack on the mill, wrote that Smith and Miller were members of the Livingston militia that conducted the siege. See Isaac Leany petition in Clark V. Johnson, ed., *Mormon Redress Petitions: Documents of the 1833–1838 Missouri Conflict* (Provo, UT: Religious Studies Center, Brigham Young University, 1992), 487.

20. Eames, quoted in *Journal History of the Church*, October 30, 1838, 11. Eames mentions White's removal to Livingston County in connection with that of George Miller and Sardius Smith. White's apostasy is briefly referred to in David Lewis, "Autobiography," manuscript, 26, Church History Library, Salt Lake City, Utah (hereafter cited as CHL); and McBride, "Autobiography," 16. John Pye, another Mormon living in nearby Breckinridge Township, also abandoned Mormonism about this same time and moved away, also probably into Livingston County. See *History of Caldwell and Livingston Counties*, 636.

21. See Amanda Smith, quoted in Emmeline B. Wells, "Amanda Smith," *Women's Exponent* 9, no. 24 (May 15, 1881), 189; and Amanda Smith petition in Johnson, *Mormon Redress Petitions*, 539; also in Joseph Smith Jr., *History of the Church of Jesus Christ of Latter-day Saints*, ed. B. H. Roberts, 2d ed., rev., 7 vols. (Salt Lake City: Deseret Book, 1971), 3:325 (hereafter cited as *History of the Church*). See also Thomas D. Casper and Jacob Foutz petitions in Johnson, *Mormon Redress Petitions*, 158, 208; also in *History of the Church*, 4:64, 68.

22. Daniel Ashby, quoted in the *Missouri Republican*, December 24, 1838, 2; spelling standardized.

23. Lewis, "Autobiography," 10; spelling standardized. Ellis Eames wrote that both he and Gilmon Merrill (Eames identified him as Gilman Merrick) lost some stock to the banditti, while Isaac Calkin and a Mormon by the name of Miller had their horses taken. Eames, quoted in *Journal History of the Church*, October 30, 1838, 11.

24. Eames, quoted in *Journal History of the Church*, October 30, 1838, 12.

25. Eames, quoted in *Journal History of the Church*, October 30, 1838, 12–13; also Lewis, "Autobiography," 11; and Isaac Leany petitions in Johnson, *Mormon Redress Petitions*, 266–267, 486. Jacob Foutz wrote that besides taking their guns and threatening to burn the mill, the marauders also took some of their horses and cattle. See Jacob Foutz petition in Johnson, *Mormon Redress Petitions*, 694.

26. Abraham Palmer to W. Taylor and S. A. Taylor, June 26, 1839, manuscript, CHL.

27. William H. Walker, *The Life Incidents and Travels of Elder William Holmes Walker and His Association with Joseph Smith the Mormon Prophet* (n. p.: Elizabeth Jane Walker Piepgrass, 1943), 6–7.

28. *History of Caldwell and Livingston Counties*, 146; and Holcombe, "The Haun's [Hawn's] Mill Massacre," 227.

29. Amanda Smith, quoted in Edward W. Tullidge, *Women of Mormondom* (New York: n. p., 1877), 121. See also Amanda Smith, quoted in Wells, "Amanda Smith," *Women's Exponent* 9, no. 22 (April 15, 1881):165; Amanda Smith petition in Johnson, *Mormon Redress Petitions*, 538; also in *History of the Church*, 3:323–324; and Philindia Myrick [Merrick] petition in Johnson, *Mormon Redress Petitions*, 505. Joseph and Jane A. Young give a similar description of their treatment in their petition in Johnson, *Mormon Redress Petitions*, 721; also *History of the Church*, 3:183. The Young petition is the source most frequently cited in the secondary sources that describe the events associated with the massacre. For a historical analysis of Young's document, see Alexander L. Baugh, "Joseph Young's Affidavit of the Massacre at Haun's [Hawn's] Mill," *BYU Studies* 38, no. 1 (1999):188–202. American historians Richard Hofstadter and Michael Wallace include Young's account in a section on religious violence in *American Violence: A Documentary History* (New York: Alfred A. Knopf, 1970), 301–304.

30. Young petition in Johnson, *Mormon Redress Petitions*, 721; also *History of the Church*, 3:183. Nathan K. Knight wrote that they actually escaped from their captors after the captors became drunk and fell asleep. See Nathan K. Knight, "Extracts from a Statement of Nathan K. Knight," in *History of Caldwell and Livingston Counties*, 157; see also Nathan Knight petition in Johnson, *Mormon Redress Petitions*, 260. The site known as Whitney's Mill was owned by Joshua Whitney, who operated a mill and a ferry on Shoal Creek farther downstream from Hawn's Mill. It was from Whitney's Mill that William Mann's company harassed Mormon settlers. Whitney was also a participant in the previously cited incident associated with Hiram Abbot. See *History of Caldwell and Livingston Counties*, 146, 701, 705, 1188. According to local history, Whitney's Mill was situated in Livingston County. See *History of Caldwell and Livingston Counties*, 146, 705. On the inside cover of *Mormon Redress Petitions*, historian Clark V. Johnson incorrectly placed the site of Whitney's Mill in Caldwell County. He perpetuated this mistake in a later publication. See the map accompanying Johnson's essay, "Northern Missouri," in *Historical Atlas of Mormonism*, ed. S. Kent Brown, Donald Q. Cannon, and Richard H. Jackson (New York: Simon and Schuster, 1994), 43.

31. Eames, quoted in *Journal History of the Church*, October 30, 1838, 12.

32. Eames, quoted in *Journal History of the Church*, October 30, 1838, 12–13.

33. Holcombe, "The Haun's [Hawn's] Mill Massacre," 226. Holcombe dates the agreement with Comstock as October 28. Margaret Foutz, a young girl at the time of the massacre, wrote that Evans met personally with Comstock. See Margaret Foutz, as quoted in Edward W. Tullidge, *The Women of Mormondom* (New York: Tullidge and crandall, 1877), 170.

34. See Isaac Leany petitions in Johnson, *Mormon Redress Petitions*, 267, 486. It was probably one of these two meetings with the Caldwell non-Mormons that David Lewis was referring to when he wrote: "A short time previous to the massacre at Shoal creek, we made peace with the mob characters living near us. . . . We met them and an agreement was entered into between us, that we would live in peace, let others do as they would." David Lewis, quoted in "A History of the Persecution of the Church of Jesus Christ of Latter-day Saints in Missouri," in *Times and Seasons* 1, no. 10 (August 1840):147.

35. This conclusion is based on the fact that many of the men who spearheaded and participated in the attack at Hawn's Mill were also members of the vigilante bands who confiscated the Mormons' weapons and took part in the peace settlements.

36. Eames, quoted in *Journal History of the Church*, 13. Concerning these negotiations, David Lewis wrote, "We then sent delegates to them to see if we could not compromise with them and live in peace, they met our delegates with guns and in a hostile manner, but finally agreed with our men that they would be at peace with us." Lewis, "Autobiography," 10; spelling standardized.

37. David Fullmer petition in Johnson, *Mormon Redress Petitions*, 451; spelling and capitalization standardized. See also Warren Foote, "Autobiography of Warren Foote," typescript, 26, Perry, Special Collections.

38. Holcombe, "The Haun's [Hawn's] Mill Massacre," 226.

39. Daniel Tyler, "Recollections of the Prophet Joseph Smith," *Juvenile Instructor* 27 (February 1, 1892):94–95. Little is known concerning John Killian, the officer mentioned by Tyler. Parley P. Pratt stated that when Hinkle was not in Far West, Killian was the officer in charge of the Mormon forces. See Parley P. Pratt, *History of the Late Persecution Inflicted by the State of Missouri Upon the Mormons* (Detroit: Dawson and Bates, Printers, 1839), 33; also in Johnson, *Mormon Redress Petitions*, 78. Sidney Rigdon also makes brief mention of Killian in connection with the Far West forces. See Sidney Rigdon petition in Johnson, *Mormon Redress Petitions*, 672–673. Tyler, Pratt, and Rigdon all indicate Killian held the rank of captain.

40. Tyler, "Recollections of the Prophet Joseph Smith," 95.

41. Lewis, "Autobiography," 11–12; spelling standardized.

42. Philo Dibble, "Philo Dibble's Narrative," in *Early Scenes in Church History: Eighth Book of the Faith-Promoting Series* (Salt Lake City: Juvenile Instructor Office, 1882), 90; reprinted in *Four Faith-Promoting Classics*, Part 4 (Salt Lake City: Bookcraft, 1968), 90; spelling standardized. In an address given by Brigham Young in 1866, he indicated that Joseph Smith instructed David Evans, the branch president at Hawn's Mill, to instruct the people in the vicinity of the settlement to move to Far West. Young was reported to have said, "Now let me make an application taking the circumstances of Haun's [Hawn's] Mill[,] that is the massacre there[,] if Brother David Evans . . . had have taken Joseph's counsel there would no person been hurt[.] I heard Joseph talk with him[,] he said gather up that people and bring them to this place [Far West] where [they would] be safe[.] Brother Evans said we are strong enough to defend ourselves and made a compromise with the mob and we are safe." Brigham Young, Remarks Given at Salt Lake City, Utah, May 20, 1866, George D. Watt Papers, Church

History Library, shorthand transcription by LaJean Purcell Carruth. So the question could be raised, did Joseph Smith instruct Jacob Hawn to tell the Saints living in the vicinity of Hawn's Mill to move to Far West, or did the Prophet instruct David Evans, the branch president? I conclude that it was Hawn, primarily because all the other sources state it was he, the most important source being that of David Lewis, who actually lived there (his property was directly adjacent to Hawn's) and who specifically indicated it was Hawn. Evans probably came at some time to Far West to counsel with Joseph Smith, which may be why Young remembered the Prophet conversing with Evans. Significantly, Watt's original longhand transcription of Young's remarks does not include any reference to David Evans. Missouri historian Return I. Holcombe wrote that after Hawn told Joseph Smith that the Saints would be willing to defend the community, the Mormon leader told them they could remain. See Holcombe, "The Haun's [Hawn's] Mill Massacre," 226. However, in light of the statements made by Mormons more familiar with the circumstances, Holcombe's commentary appears to be incorrect.

43. John D. Lee, *Mormonism Unveiled* (St. Louis, MO: Moffatt Publishing Co., 1881), 81.

44. *History of the Church*, 5:137; spelling standardized.

45. Joseph Young petition in Johnson, *Mormon Redress Petitions*, 721; spelling standardized; also *History of the Church*, 3:183.

46. Holcombe, "The Haun's [Hawn's] Mill Massacre," 226.

47. Young petition in Johnson, *Mormon Redress Petitions*, 721; also *History of the Church*, 3:183.

48. Knight, "Statement," 157. Ellis Eames wrote: "About this time a number of movers from the East came up, intending to settle in that section of the country. . . . They stopped a few days at the mills and purchased some provisions until they should find a place to settle." Eames, quoted in *Journal History of the Church*, 13. Those known to have been members of Young's company included the families of Nathan K. Knight, Warren Smith, and Levi Merrick.

49. Eames, quoted in *Journal History of the Church*, 13; Smith, quoted in Tullidge, *Women of Mormondom*, 121; Foote, "Autobiography," 26; and Artemisia Foote, "Artemisia Sidney Myers Foote's Experience in the Persecutions of the Latter Day Saints in Missouri," typescript, 1, Perry, Special Collections. James Houston was apparently absent from the community at the time of the attack.

50. Jacob Foutz and Mahlon Johnson stated there were thirty-six Mormon defenders; Isaac Leany said there were thirty-seven. See Jacob Foutz, Mahlon Johnson, and Isaac Leany petitions in Johnson, *Mormon Redress Petitions*, 694, 472, 486.

51. Holcombe, "The Haun's [Hawn's] Mill Massacre," 228; also *History of Caldwell and Livingston Counties*, 146.

52. Lee, *Mormonism Unveiled*, 78; Holcombe, "The Haun's [Hawn's] Mill Massacre," 228; and *History of Caldwell and Livingston Counties*, 147.

A Scene of Blood and Horror: The Attack on the Hawn's Mill Settlement

Alexander L. Baugh

PREPARATIONS TO ATTACK

On Monday, October 29, vigilante leaders met at the property of a man by the last name of Woolsey, situated about eight miles northeast of Hawn's Mill near present-day Breckinridge in Caldwell County; there they made final plans to attack the Mormon settlement.[1] By noon the next day, most of the men who would comprise the company had assembled near Mooresville, in Livingston County, approximately ten miles east of the mill.[2] The commander of the entire operation was Thomas Jennings, an old-time militia officer.[3] The regiment consisted of between two and three hundred men, all on horses. Most were residents of Livingston County; Daviess, Caldwell, Carrollton, and Chariton counties were also represented. The men were divided into companies, headed by Captains William O. Jennings, Nehemiah Comstock, and William Gee, all Livingston County residents.[4] An additional company led by John B. Comer was made up of men primarily, if not exclusively, from Daviess County; these men appear to have been assimilated into one or all three of the companies led by William Jennings, Comstock, and Gee.[5] Although the operation was planned under the guise of military authority and conduct, the company leaders and the

Opposite: While the men ran for the blacksmith shop, following prearranged plans, the women and children fled into the woods. The mobbers showed the fleeing women and children no mercy, and bullets whistled about them like hailstones.

Right: Today in the small town of Breckenridge, Missouri, one of the mill stones from Hawn's Mill is mounted in concrete and placed on display in the center of the community. It was near that same town of Breckenridge where men bent on murder planned their attack on the Mormons at Hawn's Mill in October 1838.

men who volunteered acted without official orders from state officials or militia authorities; it was essentially a vigilante force whose actions were clearly illegal and outside the law.

The attackers' approach to Hawn's Mill was through an open prairie along a line between Mooresville and what is today Breckinridge in Caldwell County.[6] About two miles from the mill community, they turned south. Here Colonel Jennings left James Trosper in command of a small number of men to guard a supply wagon and two Mormon prisoners who had been captured a few days earlier.[7]

THE ASSAULT

On the day of the attack, community life at the Mormon mill was going on in the usual fashion. For the most part, there was no sense of foreboding or fear. In the early afternoon, Mormon Captain David Evans and Jacob Myers Sr. returned from a meeting with Gentile leaders. This council could not have been held with the leaders of the Livingston force, since at the time they were in the process of traveling to the Mormon mill site. Thus it is probable that Evans and Myers had held the meeting with the local non-Mormon settlers living in close proximity to the community.[8] Upon his return, Evans led those who could be assembled in community prayer.[9]

David Evans, the branch president and captain over the Mormons at Hawn's Mill, returned from a meeting in which he had been negotiating peace with the local settlers just a short time before the attack on Hawn's Mill occurred.

On the afternoon of October 30, 1838, Mormon children played along the banks of Shoal Creek while their mothers watched over them and busied themselves with domestic concerns. It was a quiet autumn afternoon whose peace was suddenly shattered by the attack.

Just before the attack, children were playing along the banks of the stream; the women were busily engaged in domestic chores and making evening meal preparations, while most of the men were employed in their usual occupations—chopping and gathering wood, working in the nearby fields, or operating the mills. Hiram Abbot and Rial Ames were cutting each other's hair.[10]

Sometime between three and four p.m. the vigilante force arrived in the area, stopping just north of the mill in the heavily timbered area running about a mile and a half in width and lying a few hundred yards north of the community.[11] They were secluded by the undergrowth and were not detected until they began the actual assault. Upon emerging from the wooded area, the militia-mob advanced from three sides: Jennings aligned his men in the center directly north, while Comstock and Gee's companies took positions on the east and west.[12] The Mormons at the mill who could see the approach of the Livingston militia initially thought they were some of their brethren from Far West. However, the blackened faces, red bandanas, and overall hostile appearance soon

David Evans, courtesy of the Church History Library. *They Came Like Demons* © AD Shaw.

The mobbers divided into three lines and approached Hawn's Mill from three sides. When the Mormons discovered their presence, mob members charged down on the Mormons, shouting and shooting.

gave the attackers away, and a white flag was hoisted. Upon seeing the flag, the Missourians, knowing they had been discovered, hastened the attack.[13]

The first line, comprising sixty to seventy men, came in full gallop toward the settlement until they got within about one hundred yards of the mill, then immediately halted and dismounted.[14] Seeing the superiority of their numbers, David Evans, the community leader and Mormon captain, swung his hat, cried for peace, and called for quarter. His entreaty was not heeded. Nehemiah Comstock fired his gun, signaling his men to open fire. With the assault underway, Evans ordered the men to run to the blacksmith shop.[15]

The surprise attack threw the Mormons into an extreme state of confusion, especially the women and children, who cried and screamed in excitement and terror. Thinking first of the safety of their spouses and children, a few men directed them across a plank running along the top of the mill dam to the south bank of Shoal Creek, then encouraged them to retreat farther into the woods.[16] During the flight, the Missourians purposely fired on the innocent women and their youngsters. While running with one six-year-old daughter at her side and another year-old girl in her arms, Amanda Smith fled across the dam and up a wooded slope on the other side. "The bullets whistled by me like hailstones," she later recalled, "and cut down the bushes on all sides of me."[17] Not knowing if the Missouri ruffians would pursue them, Margaret Foutz and several other women wandered a considerable distance before they believed they were out of danger. "We ran about three miles into the woods, and there huddled together," she wrote,

"spreading what few blankets or shawls we chanced to have on the ground for the children; here we remained until two o'clock the next morning."[18] Not all of the women found refuge in the woods. Olive Eames found a cubbyhole under a bluff alongside the stream large enough to conceal herself and several children.[19] A number of other women fled to nearby cabins hoping they would not be pursued or discovered. Fortunately, nearly all the fifty women and children living in the settlement made it to safety.

The blacksmith shop where thirty-two men and four boys took shelter was only eighteen feet square. It was unfinished, with gaps between the logs and a log missing from the wall on the north side. Rather than proving to be a safe shelter, it became a slaughterhouse.

Only one woman, Mary Stedwell, was wounded in the initial assault. As the marauders made their first advance, she raised her hands pleading for peace. In doing so, she was shot in the hand. After being injured, she saw no other recourse than to run for cover with the other women and children, but she did not get far. After reaching the opposite side of the creek, and being overcome by shock and fatigue, Mary fell down behind a log, where she hoped to rest for a few moments and at the same time seclude herself from the militia. However, unknown to her, a portion of her clothing hung over the log, thus exposing her whereabouts to her attackers, who were still in range and who continued to shoot at her for some considerable time. Although she received no further wounds, when her hiding place was examined after the attack, more than twenty bullets were found lodged in the toppled trunk.[20]

As the fighting commenced, eighteen-year-old Hiram Rathbun was wounded in his right leg. In his attempt to get to safety he couldn't run very well, but fortunately his father, Robert, saw him, recognized his plight, grabbed him, put him on his back, and carried him into the woods. When he felt he was a safe distance from the fighting, Robert put Hiram on the ground then went to get help. In the meantime, Hiram passed out. When he regained consciousness, his sisters were attending to his injury. His father eventually came back, along with Hiram's uncle, and the two men took him home. Although he recovered, he was crippled for life.[21]

While the women and children scattered into the woods and nearby homes, most of the men darted into the blacksmith shop, where they had stockpiled what weapons they had.[22] The shop was approximately eighteen feet square—not very large for the thirty-two men and

The Blacksmith Shop, artist unknown, courtesy of the Church Archives, The Church of Jesus Christ of Latter-day Saints.

four boys known to have entered the structure. The shop was built of large logs, spaced some distance apart, and two windows. Because the building was still uncompleted, it had not been chinked or daubed, and there were wide cracks between each log. On the north side, one log was cut out entirely, which enabled the Mormon defenders to shoot their guns from a position inside the building. The door was located on the south, facing Shoal Creek.[23] While the Mormons believed the construction of the building would serve as an appropriate fortification, it soon proved to be more of "a slaughter-house rather than a shelter."[24] "The shop was very open," David Lewis wrote, and "each bullet that passed through these many openings was bound to prove fatal to some of us within."[25]

The Mormons held off their attackers for several minutes. However, because Colonel Jennings had organized his forces into at least two lines, after the first column positioned and fired, the second line took its place, thus allowing the first group time to reload. In this fashion, the militia was able to maintain a constant and continual conflagration upon the Mormons.[26] It did not take long for the Mormons to perceive they were not only outnumbered, but they could not successfully defend themselves from their position inside the shop. Recognizing they could resist for only so long and that complete capitulation was inevitable, Evans, who by this time had made his way into the blacksmith shop, made a second attempt to call for a cease fire. He ran out of the building, exposing himself to the enemy's barrage, "[calling] for peace and solicit[ing] them to desist." Nathan K. Knight also went out, joining Evans in supplicating for a truce, "but all to no effect."[27] During all this time, the Missourians continued their fire. In the process, Knight was shot in the right hand, which caused him to lose one finger and disable another. Rather than go back into the shop, both Knight and Evans made an attempt to escape into the woods across the creek. While Knight was making his break across the mill dam he was shot in the leg. A third bullet hit him in the back, the ball passing through his body and lodging in the pit of his stomach. Although severely wounded, he continued his escape, making his way over the hill on the other side of the stream across from the mill and running about three-quarters of a mile into the woods, where he remained until after the militia left.[28] Evans escaped unharmed.[29] The militia slowly closed in, forming a half circle on the north end of the shop and extending around the east and west sides.[30] As they did so, their fire became more deadly. Several Missourians succeeded in taking sniper positions behind logs and trees within close range and were able to discern the movements of many of the Mormon men inside. About this time the Mormons inside the blacksmith shop experienced their first injuries and casualties. David Lewis took a position by the west

The mob succeeded in advancing up to the walls of the blacksmith shop, where they were then able to fire through the cracks at point-blank range. Most of the men who tried to run from the shop were shot down.

window, but in order to shoot out, he had to step on a block. As he raised himself to the opening, he spied a Missourian who had his gun sighted directly on him, so he ducked back down and dismounted the block. No sooner had he backed down than one of his comrades stepped up to the window to shoot and was immediately gunned down and killed.[31]

The vigilante force eventually succeeded in completely overwhelming the Mormons, thus enabling a few of their men to slip under the Mormons' fire and secure positions directly outside the walls of the shop. Daniel Ashby, one of the Missourians who was ordered to move in and secure the building, observed that the man directly ahead of him had made it safely all the way to the outside wall by squatting low to the ground. He then crawled over to one of the openings where the Mormons were shooting from and sat still. Within a short time, a Mormon defender put his gun through the gap, not knowing a militiaman was pitched directly beneath his muzzle, and discharged his gun. No sooner had he drawn back his weapon, than the Missourian shoved his through the hole and fired. Within a short time "our men got possession of all the port house, [and] cracks," wrote Ashby, "and kept up such a constant fire that the Mormons could not get their guns out to shoot."[32]

"Seeing no prospect before us but death, the mob manifesting all malice possible and would not listen to our cries and seemed determined to murder us all, we thought it advisable for us to make our

The Hawn's Mill Massacre by C. A. Christensen, courtesy of the Church History Library.

escape," wrote Ellis Eames.[33] The door, situated on the south side of the shop facing the creek, was the only feasible exit, and fortunately for the Mormons, it was on the only side not directly exposed to enemy fire. However, since the Missourians were also positioned on the east and west, anyone trying to make a break would still be mostly unprotected. It was clear to the trapped men that anyone leaving would be shot at, but it appeared their only hope for survival. Hiram Abbot, Tarlton Lewis, and two others were the first to make for the woods. Abbot was hit as soon as he left the door and received a fatal wound. Tarlton Lewis, who was right on his heels, was shot through the shoulder but not seriously wounded.[34]

When George Myers was about to break outside he observed a Missourian situated behind a tree leveling his gun at him, forcing him to drop back inside the shop. Recognizing that the sniper was waiting for him to make his move, Myers employed a small diversionary tactic. Using the rifle of one of his fallen associates, he put his hat on the end, and then raised the gun so the Missourian could clearly see it. Upon seeing the hat, the attacker moved from behind the tree and fired. This gave Myers a chance to aim and fire back. In doing so he wounded the man, but it gave him the opportunity he needed to make his break. After leaving the shop, Myers was hit a little below the right shoulder blade. He made his way across the dam and up the hill to safety. He walked as far as he could, but because of the loss of blood, he was soon forced to crawl. He crawled on his hands and knees the rest of the way to his house, which was located more than a mile from the mill.[35]

While defending the shop, John Walker was hit with a

Daniel Ashby, a member of the mob at Hawn's Mill, later told how the mob "kept up such a constant fire that the Mormons could not get their guns out to shoot." He then described the attempts of the Mormons to escape the blacksmith shop, saying that "many fell in their flight." Ashby would later serve in the Missouri State Senate.

Daniel Ashby Letter, courtesy of the Missouri State Archive.

ball in the right arm. Finding it impossible to reload, and knowing he would now be of little or no help, he and another Mormon defender made a dash for safety. The two men ran a short distance down the bank of the creek, bullets whizzing around them the entire time. As the two men began to ascend the hill on the opposite bank, Walker's companion, who was just ahead of him, was shot down. Walker, seeking some sort of protection, rushed under some lumber leaning against the bank. "You are safest here," a voice calmly said to him, and although the boards afforded little protection, he remained there until the militia left. He received no other injuries.[36]

Sixty-two-year-old Thomas McBride was also wounded as he made his escape. Yet in spite of his injuries, he was able to make his way back to a deserted cabin, where he hid in the cellar. He was later found by eleven-year-old Willard Smith, still in the cellar. When the fighting broke out, Willard had made an attempt to go into the blacksmith shop with his father, Warren, and two younger brothers, Sardius and Alma, but was prevented from doing so. Seeking protection, the young boy crawled under a pile of timber, where he was shielded temporarily but was soon discovered by the militia, who began shooting at him. "I crawled out and ran into an empty house on the slope near the pond," he wrote. "Here, I found . . . Father McBride, who had been wounded and had crawled into a potato cellar under the floor of the house." He continued, "He begged for a drink of water and to be helped out of the cellar." In spite of the danger, the lad ran to the millpond, where he was deliberately fired at. "The bullets spatter[ed] in the water like hail," yet he succeeded in getting the water and returned to the cabin "without a scratch." Willard warned McBride he was sure to be discovered by the mob if he remained in the house, but the old gentleman chose to stay. Willard made him as comfortable as possible, then made his own way to safety.[37] McBride was later discovered by Jacob Rogers of Daviess County. Rogers demanded the Mormon step outside and surrender himself and his gun. McBride did so, expecting to be taken prisoner, but instead Rogers shot him in the chest with his own weapon.[38] This did not finish the old gentleman off, whereupon Rogers, using a corn cutter, brutally slashed and mutilated McBride's head, face, shoulders, and hands—nearly cutting off several fingers as well as an ear. McBride was then left lying in the creek.[39]

Willard Smith, the oldest son of Warren and Amanda Barnes Smith, attempted to enter the blacksmith shop behind his father and two younger brothers when the melee started, but his arms inexplicably flew up and prevented him from entering the shop. Three times he tried, each time with the same result. Turning away, he hid elsewhere. At the end of the day, by Divine Providence, Willard survived while his father and brother were both killed.

My Arms Flew Up © Julie Rogers; for more information, visit www.julierogersart.com.

Jacob Myers Jr. came close to experiencing a fate similar to that of McBride. In making his run for safety he received a flesh wound to his thigh, while another ball hit him between his ankle and his knee, breaking his leg and causing him to fall. This gave several ruffians time to catch up to him; one of those ruffians was apparently Jacob Rogers, who had just finished off McBride and intended to do the same to young Myers. However, just as he was about to kill Myers, one of his confederates called out to Rogers, telling him that if he killed the injured Mormon, he would shoot him. Then running up to the two men, the unknown man said that Myers "was a damned fine man for he

had ground many a grist for him." With that, Rogers left Jacob alone. Strangely enough, two members of the Livingston militia later carried Myers to his home, where they "threw him on the bed, and hurried out the doors, as though they expected to be shot the next moment."[40]

The last five Mormon men known to leave the shop were David Lewis, Isaac Leany, Jacob Potts, William Yokum, and Benjamin Lewis. David Lewis made his break alone. At first he thought he would surrender, since sometime before the attack he had been sick and was in a weakened condition, and he knew he would not be able to make a quick escape. However, after exiting, he found himself directly in the line of fire, so he immediately changed his mind, went down an embankment, crossed the stream, ascended a steep bank on the opposite side near Hawn's house, then headed south to his own home a quarter of a mile from the main community. During his retreat, due

Thomas McBride, an old man, was wounded in the initial volleys at the blacksmith shop; after being wounded, he ran and hid across Shoal Creek. Jacob Rogers, one of the mob, discovered him and brutally killed him with a corn knife.

Hawn's Mill Massacre Sketch, unknown artist; courtesy of the Church History Library.

The entire attack on the settlement at Hawn's Mill lasted about thirty to sixty minutes, and it was estimated that the mob fired some 1,600 rounds of ammunition in the murderous melee.

to his physical condition, he was unable to run, and although he was exposed to enemy fire for two hundred yards, and five shots went through his clothing, he was uninjured.[41]

Isaac Leany made a harrowing and miraculous escape. When he and his companions left the shop they were fired on at a range of only twenty to twenty-five yards. Upon making his break, he was pelted with bullets and hit several times. In spite of his injuries, he was able to make his way to the mill, where he climbed down one of the mill's timbers to the creek; then he waded through the frosty water until he came to Jacob Hawn's home, where several Mormon women had gathered. The ladies quickly ushered him into the cabin and attended briefly to his wounds. However, fearing the mob might storm the house and discover Leany, the women removed a floor board, laid Leany down in the cavity, and replaced the board securely. Here he remained until the vigilantes left, all the while suffering extreme discomfort as a result of his extensive wounds.[42] Four balls had passed entirely through his body, leaving eight holes. He was also grazed by two more bullets, resulting in flesh wounds to each arm. During his flight his buckhorn charger was shot away, as was the entire breech on his rifle. Following the ordeal, twenty-seven bullet holes were counted in his shirt and another seven in his pants.[43]

Jacob Potts, William Yokum, and Benjamin Lewis were each eventually hit by a barrage of enemy fire. After exiting the blacksmith shop, Potts was hit twice in his right leg. In spite of his injuries, he eventually made his way to David Lewis's cabin, where he borrowed a horse and then rode to his own home.[44] William Yokum fell just after he had crossed the mill dam. He was hit in two places—in his leg, which injury probably caused his fall, and in the face, as a bullet passed through his head. He miraculously recovered from his head wound, but his leg was later amputated.[45] Benjamin Lewis was mortally wounded shortly after making his break. Rockholt was at the mill; he shot long distance with a long-range rifle, shooting Lewis in the back near the shoulder blade. Although severely injured, Lewis continued on a short distance before his strength finally gave out. After the Missourians left the area, he was discovered three hundred yards from the blacksmith shop.[46]

After the last group of Mormon defenders broke out of the shop, some of Jennings's men yelled for quarter, and the Missourians finally ceased firing. Upon hearing that the gunfire had stopped, a few of the Mormon defenders who had made their way to the bank opposite the shop shot a few final rounds before turning and running on.[47] The Mormon men who escaped from the blacksmith shop did not fare well. Thirteen were wounded in their escape, and three later died as a result of their injuries. Thomas McBride was wounded and then killed, and John Walker, although wounded before he made his exit, succeeded in reaching safety. Only four Mormons—Rial Ames, Ellis Eames, David Evans, and David Lewis—escaped uninjured.

With the fighting over, several members of the Livingston regulators cautiously approached the structure to investigate and determine the extent of the Mormon losses. Inside, eight Mormons lay dead—John Byers, Elias Benner, Alexander Campbell, Josiah Fuller, John Lee, Levi N. Merrick, William Napier (also Naper), and George S. Richards. In addition, four men were wounded, and another man and three boys were uninjured, having concealed themselves as best they could, hoping they would not be discovered. Once inside, the Missourians continued their hostilities, abusing the wounded who appeared to be close to death and killing others. Three of the most severely injured were Simon Cox, Austin Hammer, and Warren Smith. Cox, the first Mormon to be wounded in the attack, received several balls in his midsection.[48] Hammer was hit in seven places, two shots having broken both of his thighs.[49] Warren Smith, who was the worst off of the three, was almost dead. Recognizing all three men would not likely live long due to the extent of their injuries, the vigilantes began stripping them of their clothing and boots. William Mann, of Mooresville Township in Livingston County, was particularly brutal with Warren Smith. While pulling off one of his boots, Mann dragged the injured man across the shop, whereupon Smith exclaimed, "Oh, you hurt me!" He then took hold of the other boot, dragging him once again until it came off. The strain was too much for the injured Mormon, and Smith soon expired.[50] Cox and Hammer were taken outside into the yard so

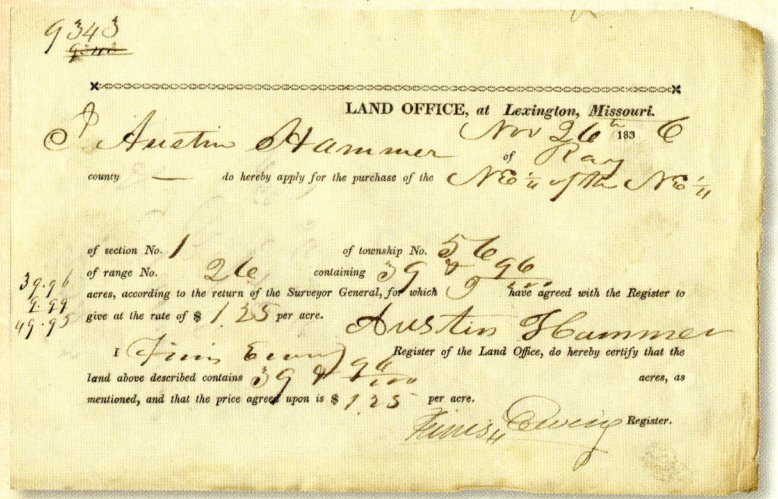

Little could Austin Hammer have imagined when he bought his land along Shoal Creek that the excitement of new beginnings would have such tragic endings. Austin Hammer was among those killed at Hawn's Mill and buried in the well.

the raiders could have more room to remove their boots and clothing. Here, the two men were left to die, although both lived for several hours afterward.[51] The dead were also stripped of their salvageable clothing and footwear.[52] While the Missourians were conducting their search of the shop, the most senseless shootings took place. At the time of the attack, three young boys had followed their fathers into the shop—Sardius (age ten) and Alma Smith (age seven), two sons of Warren Smith; and Charles Merrick (age nine), son of Levi N. Merrick. During the siege, the boys shielded themselves from the heavy gunfire by hiding beneath the furnace bellows. However, following the fight, one of the Livingston soldiers outside the shop could see where they were sequestered, and, putting his gun through a large crack, fired a shot, wounding Alma in the hip.[53] Upon further investigation while inside the building, the Missourians found all three boys. The Merrick boy tried to escape, making a break through the open door. As he ran outside, he was fired upon, receiving a load of buckshot and at least one ball, resulting in three wounds. He never recovered from his injuries and died four weeks later.[54] While a cowering and trembling Sardius pled for his life, a heartless and inhumane ruffian put the muzzle of his gun to the boy's ear, discharging his weapon at point-blank range, literally blowing a portion of his head off.[55] The third boy, Alma, though wounded, feigned he was dead, lying perfectly still until the men were gone.[56]

When the Missourians stormed the building, two Mormon men were still alive and initially eluded detection. Jacob Foutz, who had been wounded in the thigh, could not make his escape with the others, so when the ruffians came in the shop, he lay face down on the ground and pretended to be dead. His pockets were robbed, and one man put his arm under him, hoping he had a pistol he could steal. He also overheard Sardius Smith's pleadings, followed by the cracking of the guns that took the boy's life.[57] William Champlin

Austin Hammer Land Deed, courtesy of the Church History Library. *Sardius Smith* © AD Shaw.

was not only alive but was, in fact, completely unharmed. Earlier, when the decision was made to abandon the blacksmith shop, he chose to remain inside rather than face what was sure to be a barrage of bullets. To protect himself from detection, he drew several of the dead bodies on top of him to make it appear as if he were one of those killed.[58] Champlin was eventually discovered but was not harmed. A Livingston militiaman later reported that following the fight they "found one man in the house [blacksmith shop] not hurt, who had fallen down in the early part of the action, and was covered with the slain." Champlin was taken prisoner and held for three days before being released.[59]

The entire assault on the mill lasted between thirty and sixty minutes.[60] Joseph Young estimated that the Missourians shot some sixteen hundred rounds at the Mormon defenders during the attack.[61] The amount of Mormon firepower would have been considerably less, as evidenced by the fact that only three Missourians are known to have been injured in the actual encounter. John Hart, a Livingston resident, was wounded in the arm. John Renfrow had his thumb shot off. Allen England, a citizen of Daviess, was the most injured, being severely wounded in the thigh.[62]

Jacob Foutz was wounded during the assault on the blacksmith shop. Unable to escape, he pretended to be dead and was thus able to survive.

AFTERMATH

Following the attack, with the exception of a few women and children who were hiding in the woods or in an isolated cabin, the community was nearly completely deserted. The militia-mob spent about an hour plundering most of the abandoned Mormon homes and wagons, taking furniture, bedding, household articles, clothing, tools, guns, farm animals, horses, and any money they could find.[63] Olive Eames observed the mob activities from her hiding place: "I could see them go into the houses and tents, carrying out clothing and bedding." When they came to her house she saw them take some of her family's belongings, putting all that they could on her husband's horse. She believed what they wanted most was money. "What little money [I] had was hid away in my old clock," she wrote. "I supposed that too would be taken, with all my bedding."[64] The amount taken by the Livingston men was considerable. A disabled Nathan Knight observed after returning to the settlement later that evening that Jennings's men had taken nearly everything. "All of our property of every description [was gone]," he wrote, "both belonging to our camp and the settlement. . . . Hawn's house escaped their ravages, but his horses were taken from the stable. I had nothing left but a small trunk; the contents were gone except a bottle of consecrated oil, which they had left on the

Opposite Bottom: Sardius Smith hid under the bellows in the blacksmith shop in an attempt to seek safety. When members of the mob entered the shop and found him alive, one of them shot him at point-blank range in the head, killing him instantly.

After the slaughter, mob members sacked the settlement, stealing whatever they could find. They even robbed the dead of their boots and articles of clothing.

ground."65 After gathering the bounty, the Livingston marauders saddled up. As they were mounting to leave, Jacob Foutz recalled that one of their leaders yelled out, "Hurrah boys let's get out of this place."66 That evening they rode back to the Woolsey property, where they made their encampment for the night.67

The Mormons had no way of knowing what the intentions of Jennings and his men might be, and expected they would possibly return to kill or capture the remaining Mormon men who had escaped. Believing the lives of Mormon settlers living along Shoal Creek, as well as those in other isolated areas of eastern Caldwell County, were also in jeopardy, the Mormons quickly sent messengers from house to house spreading the news of the massacre and warning the Latter-day Saints to be on the alert.68 Word of the massacre reached Church leaders in Far West later the next day, October 31.69

Despite the dangers of returning to the mill, many of the women and children who had fled during the attack did return, hoping to learn

the fate or fortune of their husbands, fathers, and loved ones. Amanda Smith, one of the first on the scene, knew her husband had gone into the blacksmith shop along with the other Mormon men, but she did not know the whereabouts of her three young sons. As she approached the shop her greatest fears were confirmed. She was met by her oldest son, Willard, who had already been into the shop and was carrying the wounded Alma on his back. "They have killed my little Alma," she screamed. "No," replied Willard, "but Father and Sardius are dead." He then begged her not to enter the shop, but to attend to Alma's injury. The wounded boy was taken by his brother back to the tent that had served as a temporary shelter for the emigrant family. "Our tent had been looted, even the ticking cut and straw strewn about," Willard remembered. "Mother leveled the straw and covered it with some clothing and on this awful bed we placed Alma, cutting off his pants to determine the extent of his injury."[70] Amanda discovered that her son's entire hip—flesh, bone, and socket joint—had been completely shot away. Throughout the evening and into the morning hours, she performed a crude but effective operation using what articles were available to her. After washing the wound using a pungent lye solution, she made a thick poultice from the roots of a slippery elm tree, then filled the contusion with the dressing and covered the entire wound with a linen bandage. The next day, Amanda and her four children were invited to move into the home of another Latter-day Saint family. Here, for the next five weeks, Alma recuperated while lying flat on his stomach. The boy subsequently experienced a full and miraculous recovery.[71]

Because of darkness, the dead could not be buried and were left unattended, but the wounded were cared for. Jacob and Harriet Hawn's home served as an infirmary where several of the injured were cared for, including Austin Hammer, Nathan K. Knight, Isaac Leany, William Yokum, and John York. Hammer died that night, York the next day.[72] Nathan Knight—wounded in the hand, leg, and back—remembered the misery and suffering experienced by the wounded. "Their groans and shrieks made the night hideous and horrible beyond description," he wrote; "the women were the only ones to administer comfort during that night of desolation and suffering."[73] In reality, not much could be done other than to make the injured comfortable. Many prayers were said and some of the men received priesthood blessings. By late evening, Isaac Leany was nearly lifeless and not expected to live, having received eight critical wounds. With little hope he would ever recuperate, "the elders [prayed] for his recovery, according to the order of the Holy Priesthood," wrote John D. Lee. In spite of his condition, he

Amanda Barnes Smith spent the night of the attack tending to her son Alma. After a terrifying night, they were invited to move into the home of a fellow Latter-day Saint, where Alma could recover.

Opposite Bottom: Willard Smith was one of the first to come out of hiding after the mob departed. He entered the blacksmith shop, where he found his father and brother dead. Another brother, Alma, was badly injured but still alive. As Willard carried the injured Alma out, he met his mother and prevented her from entering the shop.

was promised through prayer and faith in God a speedy convalescence. Significantly, Leany bore testimony that upon being blessed, he had no pain whatsoever and within four weeks was completely healed.[74]

Others of the wounded were not so fortunate. Benjamin Lewis was discovered by some of the women several hundred yards from the mill. Unable to move him, they secured the help of his brother, David. Benjamin was yet alive and in his proper senses, David recalled, but he was "gasping and groaning in his blood." David rigged a slide up to a horse and moved Benjamin to his house, where he expired a few hours later.[75] Later that same evening Austin Hammer also died.[76] Simon Cox and John York died the next day (October 31), bringing the death toll to fifteen.[77] Seventeen others were known to be wounded, two of whom—Hiram Abbot and nine-year-old Charles Merrick—both died a few weeks later. The remaining fifteen eventually recovered, although Hiram Rathbun was crippled for the rest of his life. Two men, William Yokum and Jacob Myers Jr., each had a leg amputated.

On the morning of October 31, the community members undertook the gruesome responsibility of seeing to the dead. But the task of fashioning coffins or digging graves for each of the slain appeared nearly impossible under the circumstances. Late October's temperatures had been unseasonably cold, resulting in the ground being nearly completely frozen.[78] Furthermore, with so many of their numbers either dead or wounded, and with only a few able-bodied men even left in the community, it appeared the task might take several days to complete. But the Mormons felt they did not have much time. "Every moment we expected to be fired upon by the fiends who we supposed were lying in ambush waiting the first opportunity to dispatch the remaining few who had escaped the slaughter of the preceding day," wrote Amanda Smith.[79] Believing Jennings and his mob-militia were subject to return at any moment, the survivors decided to inter the bodies in the most expedient way possible.

Near the mill, an unfinished dry well had been dug measuring some twelve feet deep.[80] It was in this hole that fourteen of the fifteen who died either during the attack or shortly after were buried. Joseph Young directed the operation, assisted by a few of the women and several men, many of whom lived in the vicinity but were not present at the attack. Most of the dead were put on a plank, one at a time, then carried to the well, where the bodies were slid into the communal grave.[81] For nine-year-old Artemisia Myers, the display was horrifying: "Every time they

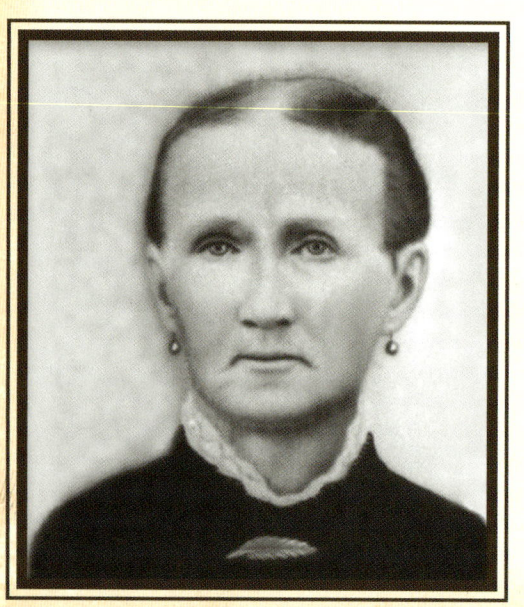

Artemisia Myers was only nine years old when she witnessed the bodies of the dead being dropped into the dry well. It was a traumatic sight that caused her to scream with each body that was so interred. She would remember that scene for the rest of her life.

Artemisia Myers, courtesy of the Church History Library.

brought one, and slid him in I screamed and cried, it was such an awful sight to see them piled in the bottom in all shapes."⁸² David Lewis recalled that this was "the most heart rending scene that my eyes ever witnessed."⁸³

The body of ten-year-old Sardius Smith was the last corpse to be put in the common sepulcher. Joseph Young was one of the men who carried the boy's body to the well, but he could not find it within himself to put the youngster in with the others, so he laid him on the ground beside the open grave. During their trek from Ohio to Missouri, the Smith family had been members of the emigrant company headed by Young, and while on their overland journey, Young had taken an interest in the boy and the two developed a close friendship. Thus when it came time to dispose of the body, the tender-hearted man could not perform the last rite. Upon learning that her son remained unburied, Amanda Smith cried, "Oh, they have left my Sardius unburied in the sun," then ran and covered her little boy's remains with a sheet. There he remained until the next day, when Amanda, along with her oldest son, Willard, returned to dispose of the body. "I threw him into this rude vault [along] with the others," she wrote, "and then covered [the grave] as well as we could with straw and earth."⁸⁴

On November 1, shortly after the communal grave had finally been covered, James McBride, the twenty-one-year-old son of the slain Thomas McBride, came to Hawn's Mill. The McBrides lived a short distance from the community, and on the day of the siege, James was to have been on guard. However, he was ill at the time, so his father volunteered to take his place and was on duty when the attack occurred. When word of the massacre reached the McBride home, James fled into the woods, believing the marauders would likely extend their hostilities against any remaining Mormon men living in the immediate area. He remained in seclusion for nearly two days, then decided to go to the mill to investigate the scene. He left a poignant recollection of his experience:

> About the first day of November, being tired of lying out in the woods, I concluded to venture a trip to the mill. I was anxious to see

Fearing that the mob would return at any moment, and with the ground frozen, the Saints decided to inter the dead in a dry well. Sardius Smith was one of the last to be placed in the well. None of the men could bring themselves to bury the boy, so his mother and brother placed the boy in what Amanda described as a "rude vault."

the grounds on which the slaughter took place; and learn if possible, the general situation of affairs.

Accordingly, with feelings that I can not here describe, I slowly wended my way to the spot.

I walked over the grounds, noticing here and there the blood stained earth—and seriously reflecting on our then sorrowful situation.

On the outside, the logs of the shop were defaced with bullet marks, and on the inside of the shop, the ground was scarcely visible for blood.

I traced the blood from the dead bodies of those who were carried and buried in the well. I went to the place and stood at the edge of the silent tomb of my beloved father. A silent prayer I offered to God, and turned away.[85]

The precise location of the well site and grave of the fourteen Mormons is no longer known.

Benjamin Lewis—the only other casualty who died immediately following the massacre—was not buried along with the others. He was buried the day after the massacre by his brother David, who "dug a hole in the ground rapt him in a sheet and without a coffin buried him."[86] The burial took place on David's property on the south side of the stream. Sometime later, Lewis's remains were exhumed and moved to a local cemetery.[87] Hiram Abbot and nine-year-old Charles Merrick, both of whom died several weeks later as a result of their injuries, were also buried separately. The whereabouts of their graves is not known.

After seeing to the dead, and fearing the possible return of the Livingston guard, many of the remaining men living in and around the community went back into temporary seclusion.[88] Later in the day of October 31, a large contingent commanded by Nehemiah Comstock did in fact return. One Mormon remembered that the triumphant marauders entered the Mormon village and "fired their guns and blowed there bugle and frightened the neighborhood, but did not kill anymore."[89] Comstock informed the residents that he and his men had come to bury the dead, but on finding the duty had already been attended to, they "expressed considerable satisfaction at having been relieved of the job."[90] Apparently on this same date, word of Boggs's "extermination order" had reached the camp of the Livingston militia, so the captain also notified the remaining Mormons of the edict, threatening them that they must either leave the state forthwith or they too would be killed.[91] Throughout the day, Comstock's men canvased eastern Caldwell County, informing other Mormon settlers

Opposite Bottom: Not every Missourian was a murderous mobber. Lucy Walker remembered a young Missouri officer who rode into their camp and led them to shelter and safety.

and emigrant companies of the governor's mandate.

Twelve-year-old Lucy Walker remembered her party being visited by one of Comstock's men. At the time, the company her family belonged to was camped a few miles from the mill. On the day of the massacre, her father had gone to the settlement just prior to the assault and was wounded in the attack. While waiting to hear word of his condition, she said that a fine-looking young Missouri officer rode into camp. Lucy was surprised by his behavior. He did not threaten the group, but told them he came as a friend in order to save them from experiencing a fate similar to those at the mill. "He referred to the dreadful scene with words of sympathy and regret," she wrote, and told them "he was forced to join the military to save his own life, but had done and would do all in his power to save the oppressed." The young man led the group to a friendlier neighborhood where they not only met up with her wounded father, but also found temporary shelter from the inclement conditions.[92]

Fourteen of the victims killed in the attack at Hawn's Mill lie interred in a well, the location of which is no longer known with certainty.

Life at the mill during the remaining months the Mormons occupied the site never returned to normal. Following the Mormon surrender, a contingent of Livingston militia occupied the site for nearly three weeks, during which time the innocent Mormon families were often treated as if they were a conquered enemy. Even after the militia disbanded, the more vile Missourians continued their harassment until the last Mormon left the premises. But there were even greater hardships; virtually every person suffered. Women who lost their husbands, as well as those wives whose husbands were wounded, suffered the most, since they not only had to care for their households, but provide for them as well. With many of their personal and household possessions taken from them and provisions and food being scarce, life during the winter of 1838–1839 became essentially day-to-day survival. Most of the families banded together until they could make arrangements to move along with the

rest of the Saints to the more welcoming locale of Illinois. By the end of February 1839, all of the Mormons had left the community.

The mob returned to the settlement the day after the attack, furthering terrorizing those left behind and occupying the settlement. It was a time of terrible suffering and trial, especially for the widows and fatherless.

I Knew Not What To Do © Meg Rieker, for more information, visit www.meganrieker.com.

NOTES

1. Return I. Holcombe [Burr Joyce], "The Haun's [Hawn's] Mill Massacre: An Incident of the 'Mormon War' in Missouri," in *St. Louis Globe-Democrat*, October 6, 1887, n. p.; also published in Joseph Smith III and Heman C. Smith, *The History of the Reorganized Church of Jesus Christ of Latter Day Saints*, 4 vols. (Independence: Herald House, 1951), 2:227 (hereafter cited as *History of the Reorganized Church*). The property likely belonged to Stephen, Thomas, or Zephaniah Woolsey, early property owners in Fairview and Breckinridge townships in eastern Caldwell County. *History of Caldwell and Livingston Counties, Missouri* (St. Louis, MO: National Historical Company, 1886), 93, 636, 962–963.

2. *History of Caldwell and Livingston Counties*, 147.

3. In the *History of Caldwell and Livingston Counties*, William O. Jennings is referred to as being the overall commander of the vigilante force. See *History of Caldwell and Livingston Counties*, 146–147. However, this was an error and was corrected in the closing pages of the book. The correction reads: "In the account of the massacre at Haun's [Hawn's] Mill, and in other pages of this volume, it is stated that the so-called Gentile forces, or State troops, were commanded by Col. Wm. O. Jennings of Livingston county. So many statements were made to the compiler to this effect that the fact was not questioned. Too late to insert the correction in the proper place, comes the assertion of two or three parties, who ought to and doubtless do know the truth of the matter, that it was Col. Thomas Jennings, the father of Wm. O. Jennings, who was the chief in command. Wm. O. Jennings was the captain of the leading company and bore a most conspicuous part, and being a prominent citizen and well known, it came to be believed, after a lapse of so many years, that he was the commander. This correction is made mainly upon the authority of Robt. Lauderdale, who was at Haun's [Hawn's] Mill." *History of Caldwell and Livingston Counties*, 1263–1264; see also Walter Williams, ed., *A History of Northwest Missouri* (Chicago and New York: Lewis Publishing Company, 1915), 560. In 1861, Thomas Jennings shot and killed two men in Chillicothe, Missouri. One was deliberate, the other accidental. He was committed to jail, escaped, was recaptured, and was tried in 1862, but was not convicted. See *History of Caldwell and Livingston Counties*, 767–771.

4. Holcombe listed William Jennings, Nehemiah Comstock, and William Gee as the three captains. See Holcombe, "The Haun's [Hawn's] Mill Massacre," 227–228. The *History of Caldwell and Livingston Counties* also names the same three men as being the captains in the operation, but additionally names Comstock, Bryan, and Mann as having been captains in other companies that operated a few days before the attack. See *History of Caldwell and Livingston Counties*, 146, 1015. Bryan and Mann likely had their own commands before the attack on the Mormon settlement, but were not selected as captains in the Hawn's Mill operation. Missouri historian Walter Williams failed to recognize this point and names Comstock, Bryan, and Mann as the three sub-commanders, with William Jennings and Gee playing prominent roles. See Williams, *History of Northwest Missouri*, 560–561. As noted, Thomas Jennings was clearly the overall commander. Mormon sources clearly indicate William Jennings, Nehemiah Comstock, and William Gee played the most prominent roles in the attack and definitely held command.

5. John B. Comer's company included forty-two men. See "Pay Roll of Captain John Comer Company of Mounted Volunteers," Adjutant-General, Mormon War, Pay Rolls, 3rd Division, Missouri Militia, documents 36–38, fd 97, Missouri State Archives, Jefferson City, Missouri. A digital transcription of the document can be found in "Soldiers' Records: War of 1812–World War I," in the Missouri Digital Heritage database collection. I acknowledge the assistance of Richard Stewart, who informed me of this significant document and collection. The record indicates that Comer's company was mustered in on October 29 and disbanded on November 3. However, no official orders or documents authorizing their callout is known to exist, evidence that the mustering was conducted by local militia leaders (perhaps by Comer himself), and not by regular state militia authorities. The fact that the company members later received pay for their services, however, should not be construed to suggest that they operated under state sanction. It appears that when state authorities distributed payments to those men who had served in the Mormon War, since the men serving in Comer's company had been expelled from Daviess County by the Mormons, Adjutant-General Gustavus A. Parsons determined that these men were entitled to some form of military pay as a means of restitution, even though they never received official orders.

6. *History of Caldwell and Livingston Counties*, 147.

7. Holcombe, "The Haun's [Hawn's] Mill Massacre," 228; and *History of Caldwell and Livingston County*, 147. The two Mormon prisoners, one of whom was named Clyde, had been members of a Mormon emigrant company passing through Livingston County and had been captured a few days before the attack. While the attack at the mill was taking place, Clyde successfully escaped. Nothing is known concerning the other Mormon prisoner. See William H. Walker, *The Life Incidents and Travels of Elder William Holmes Walker and His Association with Joseph Smith the Mormon Prophet* (n. p.: Elizabeth Jane Walker Piepgrass, 1943), 6–7.

8. See Nathan K. Knight, "Extracts from a Statement of Nathan K. Knight," in *History of Caldwell and Livingston Counties*, 157. On at least two previous occasions, Evans had met with local non-Mormon settlers residing along Shoal Creek at the home of Oliver Walker. See Isaac Leany petitions in Clark V. Johnson, ed., *Mormon Redress Petitions: Documents of the 1833–1838 Missouri Conflict* (Provo, UT: Religious Studies Center, Brigham Young University, 1992), 267, 486; and David Lewis, quoted in "A History of the Persecution of the Church of Jesus Christ of Latter-day Saints in Missouri," in *Times and Seasons* 1, no. 10 (August 1840):147. John Hammer stated that a major meeting between the Mormons and the mob leaders was to have taken place on the evening of the day of the massacre. Hammer wrote: "Some of our leading men interviewed

the mob leaders who agreed upon a certain day when they would send a committee to the mill to confer with our brethren and see if terms could be agreed upon whereby a compromise could be arranged. On the day thus fixed, being the 30th of October, a number of our brethren were at the mill hoping to have something of a reasonable talk, being of course, anxious that peace and security might be restored. With this understanding entered into, no violence from the mob party on that day was anticipated." John Hammer, quoted in Lyman Omer Littlefield, *Reminiscences of Latter-Day Saints* (Logan, UT: The Utah Journal Co., 1888), 67.

9. Amanda Smith, quoted in Edward W. Tullidge, *Women of Mormondom* (New York: Tullidge and Crandall, 1877), 121.

10. Olive Eames, quoted in *History of the Reorganized Church*, 2:234. David C. Deming petition in Johnson, *Mormon Redress Petitions*, 440; and Joseph Young petition in Johnson, *Mormon Redress Petitions*, 722; also in Joseph Smith Jr., *History of the Church of Jesus Christ of Latter-day Saints*, ed. B. H. Roberts, 2nd ed., rev., 7 vols. (Salt Lake City: Deseret Book, 1971), 3:184 (hereafter cited as *History of the Church*). For a historical analysis of Young's document, see Alexander L. Baugh, "Joseph Young's Affidavit of the Massacre at Haun's [Hawn's] Mill," *BYU Studies* 38, no. 1 (1999):188–202.

11. *History of Caldwell and Livingston Counties*, 146–147; Holcombe, "The Haun's [Hawn's] Mill Massacre," 226.

12. *History of Caldwell and Livingston Counties*, 1015.

13. Eames, quoted in *History of the Reorganized Church*, 235; David Lewis, "Autobiography," manuscript, 12, Church History Library, Salt Lake City, Utah (hereafter cited as CHL); and Hammer, quoted in Littlefield, *Reminiscences of Latter-Day Saints*, 67. For statements that the attackers had blackened faces, see Isaac Leany petition in Johnson, *Mormon Redress Petitions*, 487; Margaret Foutz, quoted in Edward W. Tullidge, *Women of Mormondom* (New York: n. p. 1877), 171; and Willard G. Smith, quoted in Jeanine Fry Ricketts, comp. and ed., *By Their Fruits: A History and Genealogy of the Fry Family of Wiltshire, England, and Their Descendants, Including the Allied Lines of Harwood, Ramsden, Toomer, Thurston, Bosen and Maddox* (Salt Lake City: n. p., n. d.), 181.

14. See Lewis, "Autobiography," 12; and Foutz, quoted in Tullidge, *Women of Mormondom*, 171. Maviah Benner said that after the attackers came into sight, a war whoop was heard. Maviah Bennor [Benner] petition in Johnson, *Mormon Redress Petitions*, 417.

15. Joseph Young petition in Johnson, *Mormon Redress Petitions*, 722; also *History of the Church*, 3:184; and Lewis, "Autobiography," 12. Lewis indicated after Evans called for quarter he neglected to give any official orders. See Lewis, "Autobiography," 12. However, George Myers specifically remembered that since all the guns were in the blacksmith shop, orders were given to run to the shop. See George Myers, quoted in Artemisia Foote, "Artemisia Sidney Myers Foote's Experience in the Persecutions of the Latter Day Saints in Missouri," typescript, 1, L. Tom Perry Special Collections, Harold B. Lee Library, Brigham Young University, Provo, Utah (hereafter cited as Perry, Special Collections). By the time the Missourians opened fire, some of the Mormons apparently had already made their way to the shop. "Thinking their movements hostile," reported Ellis Eames, "we immediately ran into the blacksmith shop for safety." Ellis Eames, quoted in *Journal History of the Church*, October 30, 1838, 13, CHL. Eames was somehow misidentified in the *Journal History* as Ellis Eamut, and is sometimes also referred to as Ellis Ames. Isaac Leany reported that the first line of Missourians fired between fifty and a hundred rounds. See Isaac Leany petition in Johnson, *Mormon Redress Petitions*, 487. In November 1838, Daniel Ashby—a resident of Chariton County, a member of the Missouri State Senate, and a Hawn's Mill participant—wrote a letter to Major-General John B. Clark wherein he reported that the Mormons fired first. However, he noted that this was told to him by those men in the line ahead of him. See Daniel Ashby to John B. Clark, November 28, 1838, *Mormon War Papers*, 1837–1841, Office of Secretary of State, Record Group 5, Missouri State Archives, Jefferson City, Missouri (hereafter cited as *MWP*); also in *Document Containing the Correspondence, Orders, &C. In Relation to the Disturbances with the Mormons; And the Evidence Given Before the Hon. Austin A. King, Judge of the Fifth Judicial Circuit of the State of Missouri, at the Court-House in Richmond, in a Criminal Court of Inquiry, Begun November 12, 1838 on the Trial of Joseph Smith, Jr., and Others, for High Treason and Other Crimes Against the State* (Fayette, MO: *Boon's Lick Democrat*, 1841), 82 (hereafter cited as *Document*). Ashby was incorrect on this account, since virtually all other sources indicate that the Missourians initiated the shooting.

16. Holcombe, "The Haun's [Hawn's] Mill Massacre," 228. Amanda Smith said that when it became apparent there would be trouble, "Our brethren shouted for the women and children to run for the woods, while they (the men) ran into an old blacksmith shop." See Amanda Smith, quoted in Emmeline B. Wells, "Amanda Smith," *Woman's Exponent* 9, no. 21 (April 1, 1881):165. See also Smith, quoted in Ricketts, *By Their Fruits*, 181. Ellis Eames wrote: "The women . . . took to flight, taking their little ones along with them and running away from the scene of murder." Eames, quoted in *Journal History of the Church*, October 30, 1838, 14.

17. Smith, quoted in Wells, "Amanda Smith," *Woman's Exponent* 9, no. 22 (April 15, 1881):173; and Amanda Smith petition in Johnson, *Mormon Redress Petitions*, 538; also in *History of the Church*, 3:324.

18. Foutz, quoted in Tullidge, *Women of Mormondom*, 171.

19. Eames, quoted in *History of the Reorganized Church*, 2:235.

20. David Lewis, quoted in "A History of the Persecution, of the Church of Jesus Christ of Latter-day Saints in Missouri," in *Times and Seasons* 1, no. 10 (August 1840): 148. Lewis also recorded that following the ordeal, fourteen bullets were removed from the log "and preserved for future generations [as a] witness." Ibid. See also Smith, quoted in Wells, "Amanda Smith," 173; Smith, quoted in Tullidge, *Women of Mormondom*, 126; and Amanda Smith petition

in Johnson, *Mormon Redress Petitions*, 538; also in *History of the Church*, 3:324.

21. Hiram Rathbun, Deposition, Temple Lot Transcript, *Church of Christ in Missouri v. Reorganized Church of Jesus Christ of Latter Day Saints*, 512–513, question 98. See also Pearl Wilcox, *The Latter Day Saints on the Missouri Frontier* (Independence, MO: by the author, 1972), 258.

22. Warren Foote, "Autobiography of Warren Foote," typescript, 26, Perry, Special Collections; and George Myers, quoted in Foote, "Artemisia Sidney Myers Foote's Experience in the Persecutions of the Latter Day Saints in Missouri," 1. Not all of the men ran into the shop. Joseph Young and David C. Deming indicated in their writings that they did not go inside and remained some distance from the action. See Joseph Young petition in Johnson, *Mormon Redress Petitions*, 722; also in *History of the Church*, 3:184–185; and David C. Deming petition in Johnson, *Mormon Redress Petitions*, 440–441. Other Mormons who apparently did not enter the blacksmith shop include James Dayley, Mahlon Johnson, William Leany, Moses Kelley, and Levi Stiltz.

23. Lewis, "Autobiography," 12; David Lewis petition in Johnson, *Mormon Redress Petitions*, 274; and Holcombe, "The Haun's [Hawn's] Mill Massacre," 228.

24. John D. Lee, *Mormonism Unveiled* (St. Louis, MO: Moffatt Publishing Co., 1881), 80.

25. Lewis, "Autobiography," 12–13; spelling standardized.

26. Daniel Ashby to John B. Clark, November 28, 1838, *MWP*; also in *Document*, 82. Ashby was in the second line.

27. Eames, quoted in *Journal History of the Church*, October 30, 1838, 13. According to Nathan Knight, while Knight and Evans were imploring for a cease fire, Knight distinctly heard someone from the ranks of the Livingston militia command the men to "kill all, spare none, and give no quarters," indicating that the attack was meant to be a whole-scale annihilation of the community rather than an attempt to bring the Mormons into subjection. See Nathan K. Knight petition in Johnson, *Mormon Redress Petitions*, 477. In writing about the massacre in 1844, six years following the massacre, James H. Hunt claimed the Mormons never called for quarter. He wrote: "It has been said by the Mormons that this was a wanton and cruel butchery—that no quarter was shown them when they called for it. . . . This we are prepared to pronounce false; the Mormons did not call for quarter, or it would have been given them." James H. Hunt, *Mormonism: Embracing the Origin, Rise and Progress of the Sect* (St. Louis: Ustick & Davies, 1844), 188–189. However, at least a dozen Mormon eyewitnesses later wrote that they called for quarters at least twice, and possibly three times. See Abner Blackburn, quoted in Will Bagley, *Frontiersman: Abner Blackburn's Narrative* (Salt Lake City: University of Utah Press, 1992), 17; Lewis, "Autobiography," 12; Smith, quoted in Wells, "Amanda Smith," *Woman's Exponent* 9, no. 22 (April 15, 1881):173; and the following petitions in Johnson, *Mormon Redress Petitions*: Jacob Foutz, 694; Moses Kelley, 474; Nathan K. Knight, 260; Isaac Leany, 267, 486–487; David Lewis, 274; Tarlton Lewis, 490; Jacob H. Potts and Levi Stiltz, 320; and Amanda Smith, 538; also in *History of the Church*, 3:324.

28. Eames, quoted in *Journal History of the Church*, October 30, 1838, 13; Knight, "Extracts from a Statement of Nathan K. Knight," 158; and Nathan K. Knight petition in Johnson, *Mormon Redress Petitions*, 477.

29. David C. Deming, who was cutting wood on the opposite side of Shoal Creek at the time of the attack, watched Evans make his escape as he made his way across the dam and through the woods. While Evans was running, Deming asked what was going on, whereupon the Mormon captain stated that the Mormon men were all being killed. David C. Deming petition in Johnson, *Mormon Redress Petitions*, 440. Holcombe reported that after escaping, Evans did not stop until he arrived at Mud Creek, a distance of seven miles. He also stated that during the entire ordeal, Evans never discharged his weapon. Holcombe, "The Haun's [Hawn's] Mill Massacre," 229.

30. Foote, "Artemisia Sidney Myers Foote's Experience in the Persecutions of the Latter Day Saints in Missouri," 1.

31. Lewis, "Autobiography," 14.

32. Daniel Ashby to John B. Clark, November 28, 1838, *MWP*; also in *Document*, 82.

33. Eames, quoted in *Journal History of the Church*, October 30, 1838, 14. David Lewis stated Hiram Abbot was the person who suggested they try to escape. See Lewis, "Autobiography," 14.

34. Lewis, "Autobiography," 14.

35. Foote, "Artemisia Sidney Myers Foote's Experience in the Persecutions of the Latter Day Saints in Missouri," 1; Warren Foote, "Autobiography," 27; and Foutz, quoted in Tullidge, *Women of Mormondom*, 172.

36. Jane Walker Smith, "Jane Walker Smith's Story," in Kate B. Carter, ed., *Our Pioneer Heritage* 19 (1976):205; and Lucy Walker Kimball, quoted in Littlefield, *Reminiscences of Latter-day Saints*, 38–39.

37. Smith, quoted in Ricketts, *By Their Fruits*, 181. After leaving McBride, Willard ran to another house close by, where he found six frightened little girls huddled together on the bed and was instrumental in getting these children to safety. Concerning this incident, he wrote: "As the bullets had followed me into this house, I said to the little girls: 'Come we must get out of here or we will all be killed.' So we ran to the millrace which we crossed on a board reaching the woods on the other side of the pond—with the mob shooting at us all the way. After our race for life, the little girls scurried off like prairie chickens into the brush and tall corn." After helping the girls to safety, Willard took shelter behind a large tree, where he watched the activities of the mob-militia until they left. Ibid.

38. *History of Caldwell and Livingston Counties*, 149; and Holcombe, "The Haun's [Hawn's] Mill Massacre," 229–230.

39. James McBride, "Autobiography of James McBride," 13, Perry, Special Collections. It is important to note that James McBride did not arrive on the scene until after his father had been interred, so his knowledge of his father's mutilated

condition was secondhand. Rebecca Judd was reported to have been an eyewitness to the killing. See Joseph Young petition in Johnson, *Mormon Redress Petitions*, 722–723; also in *History of the Church*, 3:185. David Lewis indicated that Thomas McBride received more extensive injuries than those mentioned by his son, James McBride. Lewis stated that Rogers cut off several fingers, then cut off McBride's hands, followed by his arms, and finally slashed open his skull. See Lewis, quoted in "A History of the Persecution, of the Church of Jesus Christ of Latter-day Saints in Missouri," 148–149. Shepherd P. Hutchings stated that shortly after the massacre occurred, he was taken prisoner by a group of Missourians, and Rogers was among the group. He said he heard Rogers say the following: "I . . . took a corn cutter out of the hands of one of my comrades and swore that I would bring the d—d old cuss down. I ran to him and while he (McBride) cried for mercy, I fetched him a blow which took away a part of the top of his scalp; he still cried for mercy, but I didn't care for the d—d cuss, and so I fetched him another blow over his temple, which fetched him down. I then tried to pull off his boots, as I wanted a good pair from some of the d—d Mormons." Shepherd B. Hutchings, quoted in the *Journal History of the Church*, October 30, 1838, 6. It should be noted that in several sources Thomas McBride was reported to have been a soldier in the American Revolution. This, however, is an error. The confusion apparently lies in the fact that McBride was born in 1776, the year the Revolution began, making him sixty-two years old at the time of his death. See McBride, "Autobiography," 5, 11.

40. Foote, "Artemisia Sidney Myers Foote's Experience in the Persecutions of the Latter Day Saints in Missouri," 2; also Thomas J. Kirk, *The Mormons & Missouri* (Chillicothe, MO: J. H. Darington, Printer, 1844), 43–44.

41. Lewis, "Autobiography," 15–16. In his redress petition, Lewis requested he be paid five thousand dollars, one thousand dollars for each hole in his clothing. See David Lewis petition in Johnson, *Mormon Redress Petitions*, 699.

42. McBride, "Autobiography," 13–14.

43. Isaac Leany petitions in Johnson, *Mormon Redress Petitions*, 267, 487; and William Leany, "Autobiography of William Leany," manuscript, 8–9, Perry, Special Collections. William Leany was a twin brother to Isaac. Leany described in detail the extent of his injuries: "I am well aware that this is an incredible story to tell that a man being shot four times through [the] body made his escape by flight but I have the scars to show ten in number one ball entering my body through the inside corner of my left shoulder blade came out just about two and a half or three inches below my collar bone and as far as three inches on the right of the middle of my breast another entered through the muscle under the hind part of my left arm and passed through my body and came out under the middle of my right arm another passed through my left hip on the inside or through the upper end of my hip bone another through my right hip hit the bone just about the joint glanced out through the skin and rolled down my drawers leg in to my boot these four balls made eight visible wounds with two others one across each arm." Isaac Leany petition in Johnson, *Mormon Redress Petitions*, 487; spelling standardized. On May 6, 1839, at a conference of the Church held near Quincy, Illinois, Wilford Woodruff met for the first time several of the men who were at Hawn's Mill at the time of the attack. In his journal, Woodruff recorded meeting Isaac Leany, who showed him his wounds. He wrote that Leany received all of his wounds "while he was running for his life & strange as it may appear all those wounds . . . did not lessen his speed in the least but he entirely out run his enemies & saved his life. We can only acknowledge it to be by the power & mercy of God." Wilford Woodruff, *Wilford Woodruff's Journal, 1833–1898*, ed. Scott G. Kenney, 9 vols. (Midvale, UT: Signature Books, 1983), 1:331.

44. Lewis, "Autobiography," 16; Jacob H. Potts petition in Johnson, *Mormon Redress Petitions*, 319; and Jacob H. Potts and Levi Stiltz petition in Johnson, *Mormon Redress Petitions*, 320–321.

45. Lewis, "Autobiography," 16; and Hyrum Smith petition in Johnson, *Mormon Redress Petitions*, 627; also in *History of the Church*, 3:412.

46. Lewis, "Autobiography," 16.

47. Daniel Ashby to John B. Clark, November 28, 1838, *MWP*; also in *Document*, 83.

48. Lewis, "Autobiography," 13; and Foote, "Artemisia Sidney Myers Foote's Experience in the Persecutions of the Latter Day Saints in Missouri," 2.

49. Hammer, quoted in Littlefield, *Reminiscences of Latter-Day Saints*, 67–68.

50. Smith, quoted in Tullidge, *Women of Mormondom*, 127. Following the Mormon surrender, Mann came to Far West, where he showed the boots on his own feet and boasted, "Here is a pair of boots that I pulled off before the d—d Mormon was done kicking." Ibid. See also Smith, quoted in Wells, "Amanda Smith," *Woman's Exponent*, 173; and Amanda Smith petition in Johnson, *Mormon Redress Petitions*, 538; also in *History of the Church*, 3:324. Nathan K. Knight wrote that after Smith died, the men stripped him of his hat and coat then continued "dragging him around after he was dead and kicking him." Knight, "Extracts from a Statement of Nathan K. Knight," 158.

51. Foote, "Artemisia Sidney Myers Foote's Experience in the Persecutions of the Latter Day Saints in Missouri," 2; and Hammer, quoted in Littlefield, *Reminiscences of Latter-Day Saints*, 67–68.

52. George W. Russell, a Latter-day Saint, remembered hearing a Missourian by the name of Nathan Gomer boast that he had pulled the boots off one of the dead Mormons and then put them on his own feet while sitting on the man's body. See George W. Russell, statement to George A. Smith, manuscript, 2–3, CHL.

53. Lewis, "Autobiography," 18; and Smith, quoted in Tullidge, *Women of Mormondom*, 123.

54. Holcombe, "The Haun's [Hawn's] Mill Massacre," 229; Philandia Myrick [Merrick] petition in Johnson, *Mormon Redress Petitions*, 505; and Smith, quoted in Wells, "Amanda Smith," 173. As young Merrick made his escape, those who

55. Lewis, "Autobiography," 18; and Lewis, "A History of the Persecution, of the Church of Jesus Christ of Latter-day Saints in Missouri," 148. Four men are mentioned in connection with the brutal killing of Sardius Smith. Joseph Young and Amanda Smith reported Ira Glaze was the culprit. See Joseph Young petition in Johnson, *Mormon Redress Petitions*, 723; also in *History of the Church*, 3:185; Smith, quoted in Tullidge, *Women of Mormondom*, 127. Local history attributes the killing to William Reynolds. See *History of Caldwell and Livingston Counties*, 149, n2; and Holcombe, "The Haun's [Hawn's] Mill Massacre," 229. David Lewis stated Stephen Reynolds killed the boy. See David Lewis petition in Johnson, *Mormon Redress Petitions*, 275–276; and Lewis, "A History of the Persecution, of the Church of Jesus Christ of Latter-day Saints in Missouri," 149. Nathan Knight claimed he heard Jesse Maupin claim responsibility. Nathan K. Knight petition in Johnson, *Mormon Redress Petitions*, 260; and *History of the Church*, 3:187.

56. In 1840, at the age of eight, with the assistance of his mother, Alma wrote a short petition about his ordeal during the massacre. He recorded: "I ran into a blacksmith shop where my father was. I crept under the bellows as also did my brother and another boy by the name of Charles Merrick I was wounded in the hip, my brother had his brains blown out, and the other boy received three wounds and has since died of them." Alma Smith petition in Johnson, *Mormon Redress Petitions*, 537; see also *History of the Church*, 3:186–187; spelling standardized.

57. Jacob Foutz petition in Johnson, *Mormon Redress Petitions*, 694; and Isaac Leany petition in Johnson, *Mormon Redress Petitions*, 487.

58. Isaac Leany petition in Johnson, *Mormon Redress Petitions*, 487; David Lewis petition in Johnson, *Mormon Redress Petitions*, 275; and Foutz, quoted in Tullidge, *Women of Mormondom*, 172–173.

59. Daniel Ashby to John B. Clark, November 28, 1838, *MWP*; also in *Document*, 83; Moses Kelley petition in Johnson, *Mormon Redress Petitions*, 474; and Kirk, *Mormons & Missouri*, 43.

60. David C. Deming petition in Johnson, *Mormon Redress Petitions*, 440–441.

61. Joseph Young petition in Johnson, *Mormon Redress Petitions*, 724; also in *History of the Church*, 3:186.

62. *History of Caldwell and Livingston Counties*, 150, 716, 993; and Holcombe, "The Haun's [Hawn's] Mill Massacre," 231–232. England was probably wounded by George Myers, as discussed in the text.

63. Holcombe, "The Haun's [Hawn's] Mill Massacre," 230. Several Mormons made mention in their redress petitions of the plundering activities of the militia immediately following the battle. See the following petitions in Johnson, *Mormon Redress Petitions*: Jacob Foutz, 694; Isaac Leany, 268, 487; David Lewis, 275; Mahlon Johnson, 473; Philindia Myrick [Merrick], 505; Reuben Naper, 506; Jacob H. Potts and Levi Stiltz, 320–321; and Joseph Young, 723–724; also in *History of the Church*, 3:186. See also Foutz, quoted in Tullidge, *Women of Mormondom*, 172; and Smith, quoted in Ricketts, *By Their Fruits*, 181.

64. Eames, quoted in *History of the Reorganized Church*, 2:236.

65. Knight, "Extracts from a Statement of Nathan K. Knight," 158.

66. Jacob Foutz petition in Johnson, *Mormon Redress Petitions*, 694; spelling standardized. Willard Smith reported, "After taking all the horses belonging to their victims, they rode off howling like Indians." Smith, quoted in Ricketts, *By Their Fruits*, 181.

67. Holcombe, "The Haun's [Hawn's] Mill Massacre," 230.

68. Kimball, quoted in Littlefield, *Reminiscences of Latter-day Saints*, 39–40. Ellis or Rial Eames was one of the messengers who brought word of the tragedy and warned the Mormons in the region. Abner Blackburn recalled: "Mr Eames escaped the massacre and came to our house about dark and said the Missourians were going to kill all the Mormons on Shoal Creek that night. Every one grabbed their clothes and ran for safety to the woods. The mob satiated their thirst for blood [and] retired from their glut of gore." Blackburn, quoted in Bagley, *Frontiersman*, 17.

69. See Hyrum Smith petition in Johnson, *Mormon Redress Petitions*, 627; also *History of the Church*, 3:412.

70. Smith, quoted in Ricketts, *By Their Fruits*, 182.

71. Smith, quoted in Wells, "Amanda Smith," *Woman's Exponent* 9, no. 23 (May 1, 1881):181–182. See also Smith, quoted in Tullidge, *Women of Mormondom*, 122–124, 127–128; Smith, quoted in Ricketts, *By Their Fruits*, 182–183; and Alvira Lavona Smith Hendricks, Reminiscence, manuscript, 1, Perry, Special Collections. Included with the Hendricks manuscript is a letter noting the correct authorship of the document. A bone-like gristle replaced the missing bone and socket, allowing Alma full use of his hip and leg. See also Andrew Jenson, "Alma Lamoni Smith," in *The Historical Record* 5 (December 1886):118–119.

72. Hammer, quoted in Littlefield, *Reminiscences of Latter-Day Saints*, 68. The wounded were also in other homes. Abner Blackburn, whose family lived a short distance from the mill, wrote that their home "was full of wounded and desolate families." Blackburn, quoted in Bagley, *Frontiersman*, 17; spelling standardized.

73. Knight, "Extracts from a Statement of Nathan K. Knight," 158.

74. Lee, *Mormonism Unveiled*, 80–81.

75. David Lewis petition in Johnson, *Mormon Redress Petitions*, 276; spelling standardized; and Lewis, "Autobiography," 16. While her husband was dying, Benjamin's wife loaned a horse to a young man so he could go to Far West to get help. However, en route, the young Mormon met a band of nine men, headed up by Sashiel Woods, who forced him to travel to Richmond, where they held him captive for several days, took the horse, and robbed him of several personal items.

76. Hammer, quoted in Littlefield, *Reminiscences of Latter-Day Saints*, 68.

77. Foote, "Artemisia Sidney Myers Foote's Experience in the Persecutions of the Latter Day Saints in Missouri," 2; and Lewis, "Autobiography," 17.

78. Blackburn, quoted in Bagley, *Frontiersman*, 17.

79. Smith, quoted in Tullidge, *Women of Mormondom*, 125–126.

80. Lewis, "Autobiography," 17. Warren Foote wrote that the well was on the property owned by Jacob Myers Jr. See Foote, "Autobiography," 27. LaMar C. Berrett, a former BYU professor of Church history and an authority on the Missouri period of LDS history, believed the well was on the mill property and was owned by Jacob Hawn, not Myers.

81. See Lewis, "Autobiography," 17; David Fullmer petition in Johnson, *Mormon Redress Petitions*, 452; and Holcombe, "The Haun's [Hawn's] Mill Massacre," 232.

82. Foote, "Artemisia Sidney Myers Foote's Experience in the Persecutions of the Latter Day Saints in Missouri," 2.

83. Lewis, "Autobiography," 17; spelling standardized.

84. Smith, quoted in Wells, "Amanda Smith," 182; and Smith, quoted in Tullidge, *Women of Mormondom*, 126.

85. McBride, "Autobiography," 14–15.

86. Lewis, "Autobiography," 16; spelling standardized.

87. See George Edward Anderson, Journal, Richard Neitzel Holzapfel, T. Jeffrey Cottle, and Ted D. Stoddard, eds., *Church History in Black and White: George Edward Anderson's Photographic Mission to Latter-day Saint Historical Sites* (Provo, UT: Religious Studies Center, Brigham Young University, 1995), 101.

88. Foote, "Artemisia Sidney Myers Foote's Experience in the Persecutions of the Latter Day Saints in Missouri," 2. David Lewis stated on this occasion that he and Joseph Young "went and concealed ourselves in the brush nearby, for fear they would come to my house to renew their slaughter." Lewis, "Autobiography," 20; spelling standardized.

89. Lewis petition in Johnson, *Mormon Redress Petitions*, 275; spelling standardized; Lewis "Autobiography," 19; and Lewis, quoted in "A History of the Persecution, of the Church of Jesus Christ of Latter-day Saints in Missouri," 149.

90. Holcombe, "The Haun's [Hawn's] Mill Massacre," 232.

91. Holcombe, "The Haun's [Hawn's] Mill Massacre," 232. See also Amanda Smith petition in Johnson, *Mormon Redress Petitions*, 539; also in *History of the Church*, 3:324–325; and Smith, quoted in Wells, "Amanda Smith," *Woman's Exponent* 9, no. 24 (May 15, 1881):189. Abraham Palmer stated that on the day after the massacre the mob came to him and several others and told them if they would deny their religion they could live in peace, but if they would not, they would have to leave the country or suffer death. Abraham Palmer petition in Johnson, *Mormon Redress Petitions*, 512.

92. Kimball, quoted in Littlefield, *Reminiscences of Latter-day Saints*, 40; and Walker, *Life Incidents and Travels of Elder William Holmes Walker*, 7.

5

Living with the Memory of the Hawn's Mill Massacre:
Aftermath, Exodus, and Efforts to Obtain Redress

Brent M. Rogers

In the aftermath of the bloody massacre on October 30, 1838, widespread panic spread to the towns and areas surrounding Hawn's Mill. News of the event "caused a regular stampede" among the Mormon faithful throughout Caldwell County; some women took their children in their arms, while other Church members hurriedly grabbed clothes, a loaf of bread, or a blanket and rushed into the snow and adjacent timber to hide.[1] On October 31, a messenger delivered news of the massacre to Joseph Smith, who was then at Far West, roughly sixteen miles west of the mill. News of the tragedy led to the Prophet's decision to submit and surrender to the governor's militia force at Far West. In a later history of these events, John Corrill wrote that "Smith appeared to be much alarmed, and told me to beg like a dog for peace, and afterwards said he had rather go to States-prison for twenty years, or had rather die himself than have the people exterminated." Corrill continued: "Smith said if it was the Governor's order, they would submit, and the Lord would take care of them."[2] Over the next few days, Missouri authorities arrested sixty-four Mormons, whom they took to Richmond to answer to charges in a preliminary hearing before Circuit Court Judge Austin A. King.

OCCUPATION OF THE MILL

Following the attack, Nehemiah Comstock—one of the commanders who spearheaded the assault on the Hawn's Mill settlement—and a number of his men took possession of the mill for approximately three weeks. During this time he and his men continued their plunder and harass-

> The mob occupied the settlement for three weeks following the initial attack, during which time mob members threatened and terrorized the survivors. Amanda Barnes Smith stole into a cornfield and poured out her soul to God. She was given the comfort and strength to endure.

ment, stealing food and supplies. Isaac Leany stated that Comstock's men wantonly killed livestock and robbed the people of about "a hundred bushels of wheat and about as much corn."[3] The militia also burned all the books they could find and continually threatened to burn the Mormons' homes and fields—or worse.[4]

Many women, sick or in hiding, were left exposed to all manner of hardships—they suffered from lack of food and of necessity took on all the men's daily responsibilities.[5] Life for these women and their families became essentially day-to-day survival. Margaret Foutz recalled, "During these days of danger I would sometimes have to hide my husband out in the woods and cover him with leaves."[6] Ruth Naper testified that some of the militiamen crowded into her house without her consent. One night, when her husband was not at the house, one of the men "came to my bed and laid his hand upon me which so frightened me that I made quite a noise and crept over the back side of my children." Though Ruth stated that the man "offered no further insult at the time," the invasion of her home proved to be a traumatic experience.[7] Olive Eames later remembered: "Part of the mob gathered the crops while others did the grinding, and then they sent the product home to their families, while we had to do without. They kept possession nine days, until they had stripped the fields. We had a number of hogs. They killed nine of ours while there."[8] Christiana Benner, whose husband, Elias, was killed during the attack, said that the militia robbed her of her goods, her lands, and her "companion or means of Support."[9] When Amanda Smith's grief and hardship reached a point where she could bear the oppression no longer, she went to a cornfield and poured her heart out to God. As she prayed, she heard a voice repeat to her the following verse from the beloved hymn "How Firm a Foundation":

> That soul who on Jesus hath leaned for repose,
>
> I cannot, I will not desert to its foes:
>
> That soul, though all hell should endeavor to shake,
>
> I'll never, no never, no never forsake!

From that moment on she found the strength and fortitude to take care of her injured son Alma and her other children.[10]

The Hawn's Mill victims clearly felt that their suffering was because of their religious convictions. "In this boasted land of liberty," wrote Amanda Smith, the Missouri militiamen demanded that she and her fellow religionists "deny your faith or die."[11] Others also remembered that they were told they must renounce Mormonism and deny that Joseph Smith was a prophet if they wanted to live.[12] Some of the occupying Missouri militiamen even claimed that they would let the Mormons remain on their lands and live in peace if they denied their faith. Abraham Palmer, a Church member who was living in his wagon near the mill settlement, said he was told by one militiaman, "If you will deny your faith you can live with us in peace but if you will not you must leave the County forthwith on pain of death for we will exterminate all of you that do not deny your faith men women and children."[13]

Although state authorities allowed the Mormons to remain in the state until the following spring,[14] David Lewis was told by Nehemiah Comstock that he had three options: leave the state immediately, denounce Mormonism and Joseph Smith as a prophet, or go to Richmond and stand trial for murder. Lewis told Comstock that he would not mind going to trial, because he had not violated any law: "I would not like to be tried by mob law for I know that no Mormon could have justice done to him in this state whilst their prejudices is so high."[15] As for moving out of the state immediately, Lewis added, "I told him I thought it quite a short notice to get ready to leave the county, and the weather being so cold, and robbed of all our clothing. . . . I also told him that my wife was quite sick and not able to move so soon." Lewis also feared that if he tried to leave, he would be mobbed or murdered. To ensure his safe passage, Comstock issued Lewis "a pass or ticket which would carry me safely through the state, provided I continued to travel in an eastward course and minded my own business."[16] Lewis chose to leave, but while en route east, he was detained and held prisoner by Comstock's brother Hiram, who interrogated Lewis about his escape from the blacksmiths shop during the massacre. Lewis found no remorse among the perpetrators for their involvement in the attack and the killings. Instead, they boasted of their deeds, ridiculed him, and stole his supplies before he was finally released.[17]

NEWSPAPER REPORTS OF THE MASSACRE

By late November 1838, newspapers across the country picked up the news of the horrible atrocity at Hawn's Mill. Significantly, before the reports of the massacre emerged, news releases tended to side with the Missourians' movements and labeled the Mormons as the aggressors. However, when word of the massacre got out, public opinion largely softened, and newspaper rhetoric demonstrated outrage at the incident. Some papers even called for justice in behalf of the Mormons. Although a number of the early reports were incorrect and contained inflated facts and misinformation (in some instances, Hawn's Mill was referred to as "Splawn's Mill"), even then sympathies tended to side with the Mormons.[18] For example, an account in the *Boston Liberator*

> **BUTCHERY OF THE MORMONS.**
>
> St. Louis, Nov. 12.
>
> "Further from the Mormons.—The account of a bloody butchery of *thirty-two* Mormons, on Splawn's creek, is fully confirmed. *Two children* were killed, we presume, by accident. Considerable plunder, such as beds, hats, &c., was taken from the slaughtered. Not one of the assailants was killed or hurt.
>
> "About the time of the surrender, several Mormon houses were burnt in Chariton; and one Mormon, who refused to leave, killed.
>
> "At Far West, after the surrender, a Mormon had his brains dashed out by a man who accused the Mormon of burning his house in Daviess."
>
> We copy the above paragraphs from the Gazette of Saturday evening. We are sorry to say that our own information corroborates the details. For the honor of the State we could have wished that such savage enormities had not attended a controversy in itself disgraceful enough. We understand that the company engaged in the attack at Splawn's creek was not attached to any division of the army, but was fighting on its own hook. The men were principally from Chariton county, and amongst the number was at least one member of the Legislature. The enemy had approached within eighty yards of the Mormons before they were apprized of their approach. The Mormons had their families with them, and, to preserve their lives, the men separated from them, and took refuge in a blacksmith's shop. Here they were murdered! It is said that the Mormons had arms; but it is a little singular that they should have used them so ineffectually as not to have touched one of the assailants. The latter, in some instances, placed their guns between the logs of the house, and deliberately fired at the victims within. These reports are founded upon statements of persons engaged in the attack; and, bad as they are, are not likely to be overcharged. Will the actors in the tragedy be suffered by the Courts of that district to go unpunished?—*Republican*.

By late 1838, newspapers picked up the story of the Hawn's Mill Massacre; though they often misrepresented the facts, they sided with the Mormons and condemned the Missourians—and even went as far as to condemn Governor Boggs.

acknowledged the disgraceful acts perpetrated by Missourians who participated in the killing of unarmed men and in "insulting women."[19] The *National Intelligencer*—a major Washington, DC, newspaper—ran an article entitled "Butchery of the Mormons" that gave a brief account of the bloodshed at Hawn's Mill. That article mentioned that "two children were killed," though it added its presumption that those murders were done "by accident."

The *Intelligencer*, like many other published accounts of the crime, also expressed dismay at the considerable plunder taken by Missouri militiamen from those whom they slaughtered.[20] Some newspaper accounts even attacked Governor Lilburn Boggs. A report in the *New York Sun* stated: "We are sorry to hear of the massacre of the Mormons by the armed mob; however, this violence, being the natural promptings of infuriated men, is less positively culpable than the cool ignorance and impudent, illegal assumption of the Governor of Missouri."[21]

Several newspapers expressed concern that the perpetrators of this massacre would go unpunished. The *Boston Liberator* explained that such a barbarous and bloody deed needed to be punished, because "if a mob can, with impunity, murder and rob a community of Mormons, they can, with equal impunity, murder and rob all other sects, communities and persons, who happen to be obnoxious to popular resentment for the time being. Who, then, is safe?"[22] A Cincinnati reverend by the pen name of W. H. Channing wrote an impassioned letter that was reprinted in the *Boston Courier*. Channing decried the cruelties perpetrated on this poor people, and asked readers of his letter to understand "the violations of all law, human and divine, of all right, natural and civil, of all ties of society and humanity, of all duties of justice, honor, honesty, and mercy, committed by so called freemen and Christians," that people might then "speak out for prostrate law, for liberty disgraced, for outraged man, for heaven insulted." Channing, noting the squalid conditions of Mormon women, begged for justice against the "guilty instigators and executioners of these massacres, arsons and rapes." Channing closed his letter with a call for justice: "Life cannot be restored to the murdered, nor health to the broken down in body and soul, nor peace to the bereaved; but the spoils on which robbers are now fattening, can be repaid; the loss of the destitute can be made up; the captive can be freed; and, until by legislative acts she makes redress—*Missouri is disgraced!*"[23]

EXODUS TO ILLINOIS

A small number of Latter-day Saints left Missouri in November, but the majority did not leave until February or early March 1839, when it was decided that the main body of the Church would temporarily relocate in Quincy, Illinois. In the meantime, Mormons held to the hope that they would either get their property back so that they could sell it or that the government would rescind the extermination order, but neither happened.[24] In the end, most Mormons found little or no opportunity to sell what possessions they still had. Joseph Holbrook estimated that prior to the outbreak of the Mormon War, he could have sold his property for two thousand dollars, but following the conflict he had "only 1 yoke of old oxen and 2 cows left."[25]

Amanda Smith left for Illinois on February 1, 1839, with four children under the age of twelve, including her young son Alma, whom she had nursed back to health after he was shot in the blacksmiths shop next to his father, Warren, and brother Sardius. Amanda later remembered that she and her children slept outdoors all the way to Quincy, where she "found friends who took me in and supplied my wants for a season."[26]

In a letter to the *Missouri Republican*, David R. Atchison from Clay County—a Missouri politician, a major-general in the state militia, and a Mormon sympathizer—commented on the Mormon exodus: "At least 200 women, nearly every one of whom has a family of small dependent children have been left without any one to provide for them, with no means of support, without shelter from the storm, without protection from the cold, or food to satisfy the cravings of appetite."[27] Without access to horses or wagons, many of the Saints walked in wintry conditions the entire way to Quincy. John Hammer, who was just nine years old at the time, vividly remembered the stark conditions of the forced exodus from Missouri. In a stirring account he recalled:

> When night approached we would hunt for a log or fallen

With Joseph Smith in prison and the governor's extermination order in effect, the Latter-day Saints had no choice but to flee the state. Most chose to take refuge at Quincy, Illinois.

C. C. A. Christensen (1831–1912), *Leaving Missouri* (detail), c. 1878, tempera on muslin, 78 1/8 x 114 1/8 inches, Brigham Young University Museum of Art, gift of the grandchildren of C. C. A. Christensen, 1970.

The Latter-day Saints endured terrible privation leaving Missouri in the dead of winter. There are heart-rending descriptions of women and children walking across the frozen prairie barefoot, leaving bloody footprints on the ice and snow. Among those in that exodus was Emma Smith, who braved crossing the mighty Mississippi River on the ice with a mob closely pursuing.

Opposite Top: Hyrum Smith, the Prophet's brother, left on court records in 1843 an account of the cruel and barbarous acts of the mobs at Hawn's Mill and Far West. The savagery of the account has come to define the Mormon War of 1838.

tree and if lucky enough to find one we would build fires by the sides of it. Those who had blankets or bedding camped down near enough to enjoy the warmth of the fire, which was kept burning through the entire night. Our family, as well as many others, were almost barefooted, and some had to wrap their feet in cloths in order to keep them from freezing and protect them from the sharp points of the frozen ground. This, at best, was very imperfect protection, and often the blood from our feet marked the frozen earth. My mother and sister were the only members of our family who had shoes, and these became worn out and almost useless before we reached the then hospitable shores of Illinois. All of our family except the two youngest Austin and Julian had to walk every step of the entire distance, as our one horse was not able to haul a greater load; and that was a heavy burden for the poor animal. Everything bulky or anyway heavy was discarded before starting. Such articles as my father's cooperage tools, plows and farming implements we buried in the ground, where they may have remained undiscovered to the present time. There was scarcely a day while we were on the road that it did not wither snow or rain. The nights and mornings were very cold. Considering our unsheltered and exposed condition, it is a marvel with me to this day how we endured such fatigues without being disabled by sickness, if not death.[28]

Church members found refuge and a kind reception in Quincy. As early as February 27, 1839, public meetings were held in the community, and local merchants and other individuals donated food, clothing, money, and other items to the suffering Saints.[29] By March 17, 1839, Wilford Woodruff noted that "Quincy was full of Mormons," and the next day he and several others helped move "a number of families that had Camped on the bank of the river . . . [who] were in a suffering Condition with Cold, rain & mud & some want of food."[30]

EFFORTS TO SEEK REDRESS

In March 1839, Joseph Smith addressed a letter to the Church in Quincy instructing the Saints to obtain redress through written petitions and appeals and to gather "a knowledge of all the facts and sufferings and abuses put upon them" by the state of Missouri.³¹

Both Church leaders and members quickly responded to that request. By the summer of 1839, many of the beleaguered Saints—nearly five hundred—went before an Adams County justice of the peace and gave sworn affidavits, testimonies, and petitions that detailed their suffering and enumerated their losses. Collectively, these petitions recount the trying and brutal experiences the Latter-day Saints faced in Missouri. The images they portray would later be used in efforts to obtain from the federal government redress and justice for the crimes committed against them in Missouri. The affidavits also helped invoke some of the most enduring memories of the Hawn's Mill massacre.

While on trial in Daviess County in April 1839, Hyrum Smith heard a horrifying tale that would emerge in some form in many of the histories, appeals, and redress petitions and that would forever influence Mormon memory of the Hawn's Mill massacre. According to Hyrum's 1843 testimony, the grand jury at the Mormon leaders' trial was composed of participants in the massacre, and the "same men sat as a jury in the day time, . . . were placed over us as a guard in the night time." He recalled that those men "tantalized us and boasted of their great achievements at Haun's [sic] Mills and at other places, telling us how many houses they had burned, and how many sheep, cattle, and hogs they had driven off belonging to the Mormons, and how many rapes they had committed, and what squealing and kicking there was among the damned bitches, saying that they lashed one woman upon one of the damned Mormon meeting benches, tying her hands and her feet fast, and sixteen of them abused her as much as they had a mind to, and then left her bound and exposed in that distressed condition. These fiends of the lower regions boasted of these acts of barbarity, and tantalized our feelings with them for ten days."³² Though it is not known

From Liberty Jail the Prophet Joseph Smith instructed the Saints in this letter to gather "a knowledge of all the facts and sufferings and abuses put upon them." This resulted in nearly five hundred sworn affidavits attesting to their sufferings.

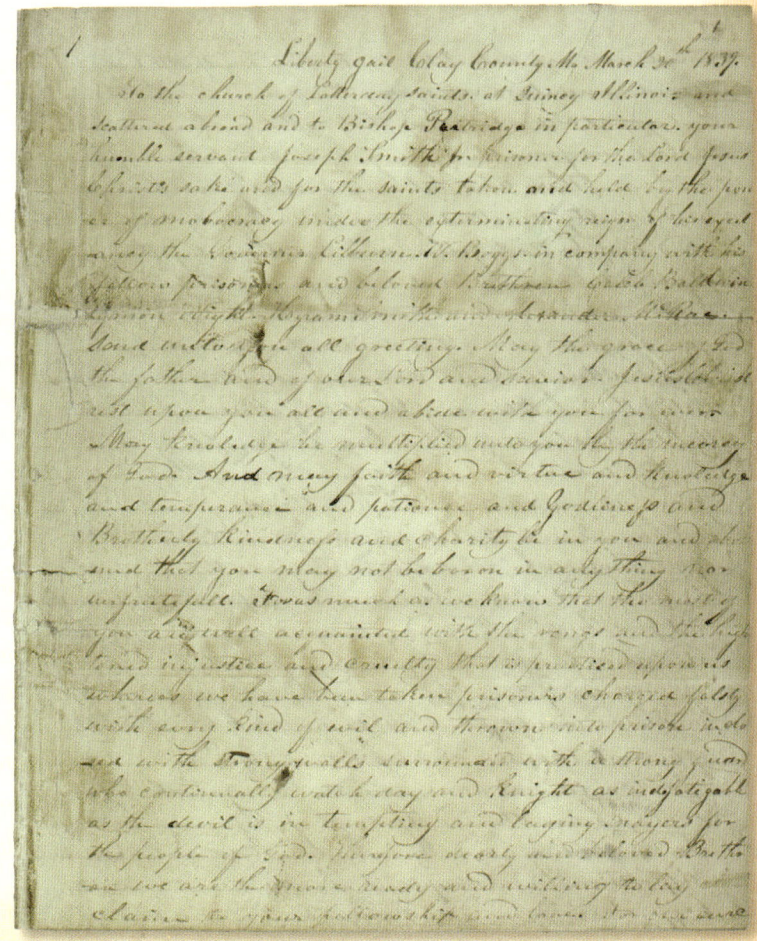

This account of the Missouri persecutions was written by Bishop Edward Partridge and was printed in three installments in the *Times and Seasons* newspaper in Nauvoo.

for certain who among the Mormon women was victimized by Missouri militiamen at Hawn's Mill, David Lewis similarly recalled that on the day of the massacre some women "were brutally insulted and abused" by their attackers.[33] Accounts of women being molested and maltreated became a rallying cry for Mormon men in their efforts to seek redress and justice against the state of Missouri. The words *rape, ravishing, insulting,* or *abusing* were used in many, if not most, of the later accounts to describe the treatment of women at Hawn's Mill and in Missouri generally.

Just a little more than a year after the Hawn's Mill massacre, while still suffering the effects of the violence in Missouri, the Saints took up pen and paper, turning the mental, emotional, and physical trauma into rhetorically driven accounts of carnage and agony. They addressed their writings to a national audience in hopes of obtaining legal redress and financial compensation from the federal government. Both Church leaders and members quickly responded to that request. Edward Partridge wrote an account that became the first three installments of "A History of the Persecution, of the Church of Jesus Christ, of Latter Day Saints in Missouri" that appeared in the *Times and Seasons* beginning in December 1839. In that same issue of the *Times and Seasons,* Eliza Snow encouraged Mormon women to think of the widows who had lost their loved ones at Hawn's Mill but to realize that those women did not lose hope or faith, though she acknowledged the sorrow she felt when remembering that emblematic event of the Missouri persecutions.[34]

Sidney Rigdon wrote a lengthy manuscript that was approved by a Church conference on November 1, 1839, and that was published as *An Appeal to the American People.* Rigdon's account of the "horrid and soul-thrilling" events at Hawn's Mill included eyewitness reports by four survivors: Joseph and Jane A. Young, David Lewis, and Amanda Barnes Smith.[35] These testimonies and other accounts surrounding the tragedy made up about twelve pages of Rigdon's eighty-four-page published history.

Still another history, titled *Expulsion of the Mormons,* was written by John P. Greene, who then went on a tour of the eastern cities to raise awareness and inform citizens of the horrors of the Mormons' Missouri experience. At a public meeting in Cincinnati on June 17,

1839, Greene recounted the murderous attack at Hawn's Mill and emphasized the killing of young boys, the suffering of women, and the plundering done by the militia. The *New York Spectator*, having reprinted a report from a Cincinnati newspaper, called Greene's narrative "indeed a tale of woe and suffering at which the heart sickens."[36] On September 16, 1839, Greene was in New York City, where he gave a speech to a large crowd at the National Hall. According to the *New York Morning Herald*'s coverage, Greene provided the horrifying details of the militia's massacre of Mormons "who were peaceably encamped on Shoal Creek, near Far West. This tragedy was conducted in the most brutal and savage manner."

Greene described the terrible and gruesome condition of the Mormons during the militia's occupation in the massacre's aftermath, but the paper would not comment any further except to say that the "scene that presented itself after the massacre, to the widows and orphans of the killed, is beyond description."[37] Parley P. Pratt later wrote that through such histories and appeals, the Saints "fondly hope that the coming generation in those two states will go to school and learn that the laws and constitutions of the United States do not result, when properly administered, in murder, plunder, robbery, house-burning, rape, and exile."[38]

By the fall of 1839, Joseph Smith was ready to take the case of his people to the U.S. federal government. With copies in hand of the nearly five hundred sworn affidavits made in Adams County earlier that year, and a petition to Congress describing the Mormon sufferings, he left for Washington, DC, with Elias Higbee and Sidney Rigdon on October 29, 1839. Though Rigdon became ill along the way and briefly returned to Illinois, the Prophet and Higbee continued on, arriving in Washington on November 28, 1839. U.S. President Martin Van Buren met with the men the next day. Smith and Higbee presented the president several documents, including a letter from James Adams of Springfield, Illinois. Adams, in introducing why the men were in the nation's capital, wrote, "Their business is to seek redress for the recent outrages committed on them and their property in Missouri. Those outrages are unparalleled in the annals of civilized communities."[39] After browsing through a few of the documents presented, Van Buren told Smith and Higbee that the federal government had no jurisdiction

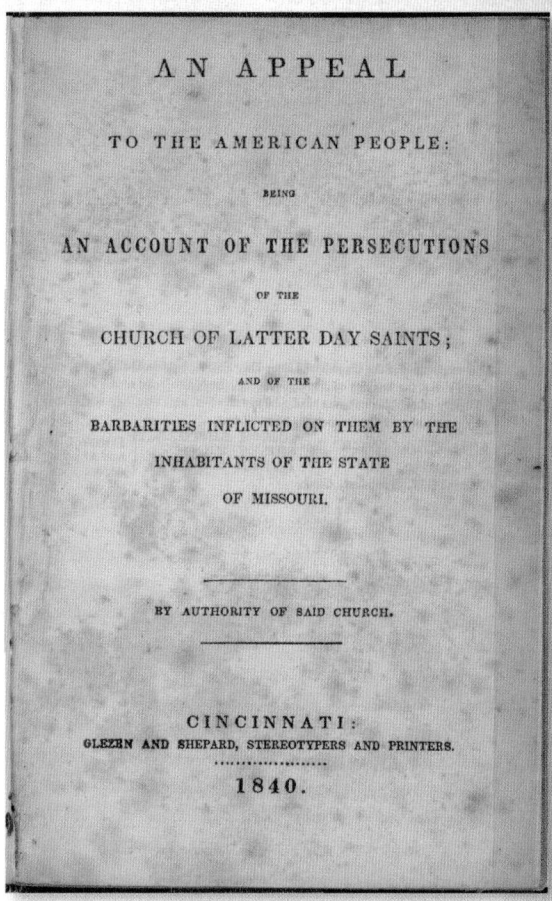

In this Church-sanctioned publication, Sidney Rigdon described at length the "horrid and soul-thrilling" events at Hawn's Mill.

> ## FACTS
> RELATIVE TO THE
> ## EXPULSION OF THE MORMONS
> FROM THE STATE OF MISSOURI.
>
> ---
>
> From the Quincy (Illinois) Argus, March 16, 1839.
> ### THE MORMONS, OR LATTER DAY SAINTS.
>
> We give in to-day's paper the details of the recent bloody tragedy acted in Missouri—the details of a scene of terror and blood unparalleled in the annals of modern, and under the circumstances of the case, in ancient history—a tragedy of so deep, and fearful, and absorbing interest, that the very life-blood of the heart is chilled at the simple contemplation. We are prompted to ask ourselves if it be really *true*, that we are living in an enlightened, a humane and civilized age—in an age and quarter of the world boasting of its progress in every thing good, and great, and honorable, and virtuous, and high-minded—in a country of which, as American citizens, we could be proud—whether we are living under a *Constitution and Laws*, or have not rather returned to the *ruthless* times of the *stern Attila*—to the times of the fiery Hun, when the sword and flame ravaged the fair fields of Italy and Europe, and the darkest passions held full revel in all the revolting scenes of unchecked brutality, and unbridled desire?
>
> We have no language sufficiently strong for the expression of our indignation and shame at the recent transaction in a sister State—and that State MISSOURI—a State of which we had long been proud, alike for her men and history, but now so *fallen*, that we could wish her star stricken out from the bright constellation of the Union. We say we know of no language sufficiently strong for the expression of our shame and abhorrence of her recent conduct. She has written her own character in *letters of blood*—and stained it by acts of merciless cruelty and brutality that the waters of ages cannot efface. It will be observed that an organized mob aided by many of the civil and military officers of Missouri, with Gov. Boggs at their head, have been the prominent actors in this business, incited too, it appears, against the Mormons by political hatred, and by the additional motives of plunder and revenge. They have but too well put in execution their threats of extermination and expulsion, and fully
>
> A 2

John P. Greene authored this account of the Missouri persecutions, and with it traveled the eastern United States seeking to inform and raise public awareness of what the Mormons had unjustly endured in Missouri.

and could provide no justice or redress because the persecution incidents in Missouri were a state matter. The meeting ended abruptly with not even a word of support or encouragement from the nation's highest executive.[40]

In early 1840, Porter Rockwell and Robert Foster accompanied Sidney Rigdon to Washington. These men joined Joseph Smith and Elias Higbee as they proceeded with the second phase of their attempt to obtain redress by presenting their petition, or memorial, to Congress. Of all the atrocities committed by the Missouri militia—the houses burned, property destroyed, and victims robbed, raped, and murdered—the petition highlighted "one instance only"—the Hawn's Mill massacre. The concluding paragraph of that petition to Congress is especially poignant because it contrasted Mormon losses and their plea for redress with the constitutional guarantees of life, liberty, property, and religious freedom, fundamental American rights that had been taken from them in Missouri:

> The Mormons numbering fifteen thousand souls have been driven from their homes in Missouri; property to the value of two millions of dollars has been taken from them or destroyed; some of their brethren have been murdered; some wounded and others beaten with stripes; the chastity of their wives and daughters inhumanly violated; all driven forth as wanderers, and many, very many, broken hearts and pennyless. The loss of property they do not so much deplore, as the mental and bodily sufferings to which they have been subjected; and thus far without redress. They are human beings, possessed of human feelings, and human sympathies. Their agony of soul for their suffering women and children was the bitterest drop in the cup of their sorrows. For these wrongs and sufferings, the Mormons, as American citizens, ask; *is there no redress*? Yet, of all these rights and immunities, the Mormons have been deprived. They have, without a just cause; without the form of trial; been deprived of life, liberty and property. They have been driven from the State of Missouri at the point of the bayonet and treated worse than a foreign enemy; they have been beaten with stripes as slaves; and threatened with destruction if they should ever venture to return; Those, who

should have protected them, have become their most relentless persecutors; and what are the Mormons to do? It is the theory of our Constitution and laws, that, for the violation of every legal right, there is provided a legal remedy. For ourselves we see no redress, unless it be awarded by the Congress of the United States.[41]

Unfortunately, Congress would not allow the Mormon men to verbally present their petition. Instead, the Senate referred the whole matter to its Judiciary Committee, which examined the written petition but took no action. Instead, the committee gave its opinion that "the case presented for their investigation is not such a one as will justify or authorize any interposition by this Government."[42] Not even the disturbing account of the Hawn's Mill massacre could entice the committee to sympathize with the mistreated Saints. Like the president, the Senate committee indicated that the federal government did not have jurisdiction over the matter. Thus, Joseph Smith and his companions were left to return to Illinois empty-handed and frustrated.

In October 1840, Joseph Smith proposed that a new committee, again led by Elias Higbee, continue the efforts to obtain redress for the wrongs sustained in Missouri. The outcome of Higbee's efforts once again proved unsuccessful, but Church leaders remained persistent. A second memorial was written, though nearly identical to the first and including the same Hawn's Mill account. Church leaders again took the petition to Washington in January 1842. This petition ended like the first, with the following plea: "For ourselves we see no redress, unless it be awarded by the Congress of the United States. And here we make our appeal, as *American citizens*, as *Christians*, and as men, believing that the high sense of justice which exists in your honourable bodies will not allow such oppression to be practised upon any portion of the citizens of this vast republic with impunity; but that some measure which your wisdom may dictate may be taken, so that the great body of people who have been thus abused may have redress for the wrongs which they have suffered. And to your decision they look with confidence; hoping it may be such as shall tend to dry up the tear of the widow and orphan, and again place in situations of peace those who have been driven from their homes, and have had to

In late 1839, Joseph Smith and Elias Higbee traveled to Washington, DC, where they presented to United States President Martin Van Buren the Saints' affidavits of their sufferings and losses in Missouri. Van Buren is reported to have said, "Your cause is just, but I can do nothing for you." His abrupt dismissal effectually and callously turned a blind eye on all that the Mormons had endured in Missouri.

Martin Van Buren, courtesy of the Library of Congress.

After repeated failed attempts to seek redress at the hands of the United States government, members of the Church drafted letters to the citizens of their home states to raise awareness of what had happened to them in Missouri. This account was written by Benjamin Andrews to the people of the state of Maine.

Opposite Bottom: Sidney Rigdon, first counselor in the First Presidency, wrote directly to the legislature of his home state of Pennsylvania. He described the suffering of the Latter-day Saint women in Missouri and appealed to the Pennsylvanians' sense of decency and chivalry for aid. There was no response. All appeals at all levels for redress were ultimately brushed aside.

wade through scenes of sorrow and distress."[43] Congress again took no action.

In late 1843 and early 1844, the Church's leadership continued, largely undeterred, to seek redress, and began thinking of additional ways to raise awareness of their plight and gain support for their petitions. Joseph Smith wrote letters to potential U.S. presidential candidates and again petitioned Congress with a third appeal—this time signed by more than 3,400 individuals—for support, justice, and compensation. On November 29, 1843, the Mormon leader spoke to a gathering of Nauvoo citizens and encouraged "every man in the meeting who could wield a pen [to] write an address" to the state of his birth.[44] Those addresses were designed to appeal to the precepts of equality and human rights guaranteed to American citizens that Church members felt were lacking in their experiences in Missouri and in their previous efforts to obtain redress from Missouri and the federal government. To emphasize the Mormon struggle, some of the appeals written by individuals invoked the blood and groans of those who suffered at Hawn's Mill.[45] Benjamin Andrews, in his written appeal to the state of Maine, underscored the Missourians' barbaric acts. He described the slaughter of men and children and the subsequent forced removal of hundreds of destitute women and little children survivors, who were left to brave "the winter blasts in a naked situation" and in danger of being "hurried . . . to a premature grave." He also recounted the many efforts the Saints had undertaken to obtain redress. "We have sought for justice in the courts of that state," he wrote, and "we have presented our memorial to the legislature," and to the federal government, all to no avail. Andrews concluded with a humble prayer that his religious fellows would receive a "restoration of our property and our rights as American citizens."[46]

In his appeal to the state of Massachusetts, Phineas Richards detailed the loss of his teenage son, George S. Richards, also a Massachusetts native, who was killed at Hawn's Mill. Phineas, who was not in Missouri at the time of the massacre, included the text of Joseph Young's 1839 affidavit to depict the Hawn's Mill murders in great detail. His appeal then cried out: "Is this the boasted land of liberty? Of equal rights and of religious toleration? . . . I appeal for assistance, because my sons' blood, with that of hundreds of others, who have fallen by the violence of the mobocrats of Missouri, cries to heaven for vengeance to be poured out upon that guilty and blood stained State."⁴⁷

The men and boys killed and the women abused at Hawn's Mill on October 30, 1838, were remembered by Church members as martyrs. Benjamin Andrews wrote: "We can never forget the blood of our brethren, so wantonly lavished to satisfy the infernal thirsts of men, as heinous to the righteous, as the fiends of hell. Were we to forget them, heaven itself would upbraid us. The immortal shades of our martyred brethren would spurn us from their presence."⁴⁸ Four years removed from his writing of *An Appeal to the American People*, Sidney Rigdon wrote another, more succinct, appeal directly to the legislature of Pennsylvania. Calling on man's natural and cultural instinct to protect women, Rigdon demanded: "What crime can any man commit, it matters not how flagrant, which can, according to the laws of the civilized world, subject his wife to insult, his daughters to rape, his property to public plunder, his children to starvation, and himself and family to exile." He emphasized the abuse of women who "were insulted and ravished," and with their children "driven into the prairies, and made to suffer all the indignities that the most brutal barbarity could inflict." Rigdon, like Andrews, narrated the history of the Saints' attempts to gain redress before closing with the plea that American citizens did not deserve to suffer from such inhumane injustice.⁴⁹ In spite of the Latter-day Saints' constant and repeated attempts to gain justice, compensation, and sympathy for the Missouri violence they endured, the U.S. federal government—the entity responsible for protecting American citizens and ensuring their inalienable rights—failed to assist the Mormon people.

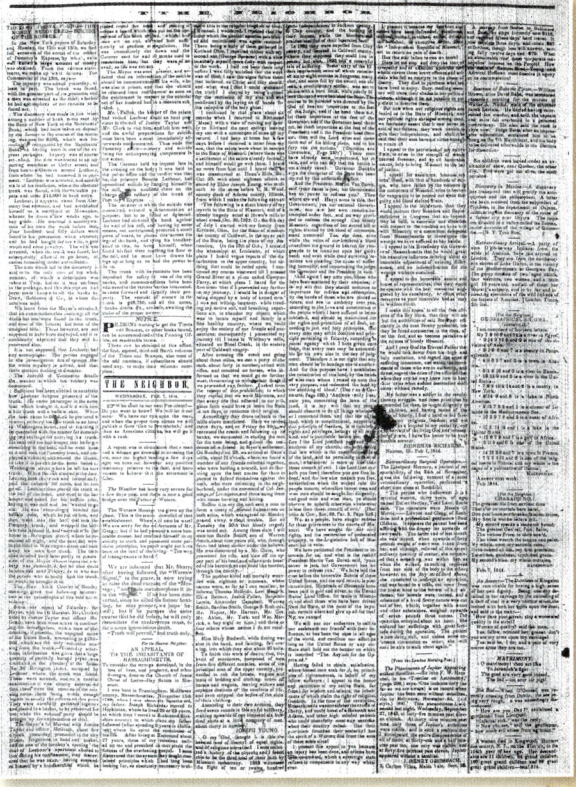

Phineas Richards was not in Missouri at the time of the massacre, but his son George was, and lost his life to the mobs. Phineas's impassioned plea for assistance and justice went unanswered.

THE HAWN'S MILL MASSACRE IN MORMON MEMORY

The Hawn's Mill atrocity continued to influence Mormon memory and helped forge Mormon resolve to protect themselves decades later. For example, during the Utah War of 1857–1858, Mormon leaders

predicted "scenes of rapine and plunder" as the U.S. troops approached Utah Territory. They believed that the federal government had sent a soldiery to the territory to reenact "the horrid scenes of Missouri and Illinois."[50] Brigham Young, in particular, feared that disease, pollution, and the debauching of "our wives and daughters" would occur once the troops arrived in the territory.[51] They believed that the troops came with the objective "to destroy the leaders of our people" and that they threatened "to take our lives and to sport, at pleasure, with our wives and daughters."[52] U.S. Army officer John Wolcott Phelps also suggested that those in the Mormon army "had been told and believed that we were a mob coming upon them to destroy both women and children."[53] The memory and fear of another Mormon War and Hawn's Mill massacre appears to have remained fresh in the Mormon collective memory during this mid-nineteenth-century episode.

During the Utah War, in early January 1858, Mormon petitioners sent yet another memorial to Washington. The Mormon memorial asked Congress to include Utah as a free and self-governing entity because the territory's citizens had demonstrated their love of liberty and willingness to uphold U.S. constitutional rights even while they believed those same rights had been denied them in Missouri. The Mormons' request, like their earlier petitions seeking justice and redress for the crimes perpetrated against them in Missouri, ended powerfully and concisely: "Give us our *constitutional rights*, and we are at home."[54] The memorial reached Washington in the spring, but like earlier Mormon appeals, it received little attention in the halls of Congress.

For Church members today, the Hawn's Mill massacre and Missouri violence generally continue

Memories of Hawn's Mill and the Mormon War of 1838 greatly influenced the judgment of the Saints in 1857–1858, when they learned that a federal army was on its way to Utah to put down a supposed rebellion. The Mormons were resolutely determined to protect their families and not to be abused again at the hands of the government, as they had been so many times before.

to evoke powerful emotions of disgrace and injustice. Some of the most important texts in Mormon history were created in the context of the massacre and its aftermath. These writings, and the associated efforts to obtain redress and justice, helped create a shared memory for the Latter-day Saint people, who were willing to suffer inequality and endure intense trials for their faith and belief. That faith demonstrated by the men, women, and children who did not deny their religious convictions to save themselves from cruelty and deprivation in the aftermath of the Hawn's Mill massacre serves as yet another testimony of the truthfulness of the Restoration. Their sacrifices, in addition to the sacrifices experienced by all the Latter-day Saints who endured the Missouri persecutions, should be remembered, understood, and memorialized with compassion and charity.

Opposite Bottom: What happened at Hawn's Mill was a tragedy of epic proportions that has in part defined the Latter-day Saints as a people, not just because of the injustice of the event, but more so because of the manner in which the Saints heroically rose above it and went on. Today the telling of that touching story reveals anew an endearing legacy of faith, sacrifice, and martyrdom for the cause of Christ.

NOTES

1. Lucy Walker Kimball, quoted in Lyman Omer Littlefield, *Reminiscences of Latter-day Saints* (Logan, UT: The Utah Journal Co., 1888), 39–40.

2. See John Corrill, *A Brief History of the Church of Christ of Latter Day* (St. Louis: Printed for the Author, 1839), 41, 42; also in Karen Lynn Davidson, Richard L. Jensen, and David J. Whitaker, eds., *Histories 2, Assigned Histories, 1831–1847*, vol. 2 of the Histories series of *The Joseph Smith Papers*, eds. Dean C. Jessee, Ronald K. Esplin, and Richard Lyman Bushman (Salt Lake City: The Church Historians Press, 2012), 183, 186 (hereafter cited as *JSP*, H2).

3. Isaac Leany petition in Clark V. Johnson, ed., *Mormon Redress Petitions: Documents of the 1833–1838 Missouri Conflict* (Provo, UT: Religious Studies Center, Brigham Young University, 1992), 268.

4. David Lewis, quoted in "A History of the Persecution, of the Church of Jesus Christ of Latter-day Saints in Missouri," in *Times and Seasons* 1, no. 10 (August 1840):149–150; also in *JSP*, H2:269.

5. Leany petition in Johnson, *Missouri Redress Petitions*, 268. See also Reburn I. Holcombe [Burr Joyce], "The Haun's [Hawn's] Mill Massacre: An Incident of the 'Mormon War' in Missouri," in *St. Louis Globe-Democrat*, October 6, 1887, n. p.; also published in Joseph Smith III and Heman C. Smith, *The History of the Reorganized Church of Jesus Christ of Latter Day Saints*, 4 vols. (Independence: Herald House, 1951), 2:232. Holcombe wrote this narrative under the pen name of Burr Joyce. See also Olive Eames [Ames], quoted in Joseph Smith III and Heman C. Smith, *The History of the Reorganized Church of Jesus Christ of Latter Day Saints* 2:236.

6. Margaret Foutz, quoted in Edward W. Tullidge, *Women of Mormondom* (New York: Tullidge and Crandall, 1877), 174.

7. Ruth Napier [Naper] petition in Johnson, *Mormon Redress Petitions*, 296.

8. Eames, quoted in *History of the Reorganized Church of Jesus Christ of Latter Day Saints*, 2:236.

9. Christiana Benner petition in Johnson, *Mormon Redress Petitions*, 136.

10. Smith, quoted in Tullidge, *Women of Mormondom*, 129–130. The lines come from the seventh stanza of the hymn, "How Firm a Foundation," a hymn that was included in the 1835 Mormon hymnal. See "Hymn 82," in *A Collection of Sacred Hymns for the Church of the Latter Day Saints* (Kirtland, OH: F. G. Williams & Co., 1835), 112–113. The wording given by Amanda in *Women of Mormondom* differs slightly from the original.

11. Amanda Smith, quoted in Holcombe, "The Haun's [Hawn's] Mill Massacre," 233.

12. Lewis, quoted in "A History of the Persecution, of the Church of Jesus Christ of Latter-day Saints in Missouri," 150; also in *JSP*, H2:269.

13. Abraham Palmer petition in Johnson, *Mormon Redress Petitions*, 512.

14. Lilburn W. Boggs to John B. Clark, November 10, 1838, *Mormon War Papers, 1837–1841*, Office of Secretary of State, Record Group 5, Missouri State Archives, Jefferson City, Missouri (hereafter cited as MWP); also in *Document Containing the Correspondence, Orders, &C. In Relation to the Disturbances with the Mormons; And the Evidence Given Before the Hon. Austin A. King, Judge of the Fifth Judicial Circuit of the State of Missouri, at the Court-House in Richmond, in a Criminal Court of Inquiry, Begun November 12, 1838 on the Trial of Joseph Smith, Jr., and Others, for High Treason and Other Crimes Against the State* (Fayette, MO: Boon's Lick Democrat, 1841), 66 (hereafter cited as *Document*). See also "A History of the Persecution, of the Church of Jesus Christ, of Latter-day Saints in Missouri," *Times and Seasons* 1, no. 9 (July 1840):130; also in *JSP*, H2:257.

15. David Lewis, "Autobiography," manuscript, 20, Church History Library, Salt Lake City, Utah; spelling standardized (hereafter cited as CHL).

16. Lewis, quoted in "A History of the Persecution, of the Church of Jesus Christ, of Latter-day Saints in Missouri," 150; also in *JSP*, H2:269–270.

17. David Lewis, Petition, in Johnson, *Mormon Redress Petitions*, 278.

18. See "From the Baltimore Sun of this Morning. THE MORMON WAR ENDED. Reports of a horrid Massacre," *The Globe* (Washington, DC), November 20, 1838, n. p.; and "The Mormon War Ended," *Vermont Chronicle*, November 28, 1838, 3.

19. "Miscellaneous: Treatment of the Mormons—Even-handed Justice," *Boston Liberator*, December 28, 1838, 4.

20. "Butchery of the Mormons," *National Daily Intelligencer*, November 24, 1838, 3.

21. Parley P. Pratt, *History of the Late Persecution Inflicted by the State of Missouri upon the Mormons* (Detroit: Dawson & Bates, Printers, 1839), 75.

22. "Miscellaneous: Treatment of the Mormons—Even-handed Justice," 4.

23. W. H. Channing, "Outrages of Missouri Mobs on Mormons," *Boston Courier*, July 22, 1839, 1.

24. William G. Hartley, "'Almost Too Intolerable a Burthen:' The Winter Exodus from Missouri, 1838–39," *Journal of Mormon History* 18 (Fall 1992):24; see Foutz, quoted in Edward W. Tullidge, *Women of Mormondom*, 174.

25. Joseph Holbrook, "The Life of Joseph Holbrook, 1806–1871," typescript, 46, L. Tom Perry Special Collections, Harold B. Lee Library, Brigham Young University, Provo, Utah (hereafter cited as Perry, Special Collections).

26. Amanda Smith, quoted in Emmeline B. Wells, "Amanda Smith," *Woman's Exponent* 9, no. 24 (May 15, 1881):189.

27. "Letter to the Editor," *Missouri Republican*, December 7, 1838, 2.

28. John Hammer, quoted in Littlefield, *Reminiscences of Latterday Saints*, 72–73.

29. "Editorial," *Quincy Whig*, March 2, 1839, 2; "The Mormons," *Quincy Whig*, March 16, 1839, 1.

30. Wilford Woodruff, *Wilford Woodruff's Journal, 1833–1898*, ed. Scott G. Kenney, 9 vols. (Midvale, UT: Signature Books, 1983), 1:322.

31. Joseph Smith and others to Church Members and Edward Partridge, March 20, 1839, manuscript, pt. 2, 5 [D&C 123:1], *Joseph Smith Papers*, Revelations Collection, CHL; spelling standardized.

32. Hyrum Smith, "Testimony," July 1, 1843, Nauvoo City Records, CHL; see also Mosiah L. Hancock, "The Life and Journal of Mosiah Lyman Hancock," typescript, 12, Perry, Special Collections.

33. Lewis, quoted in "A History of the Persecution, of the Church of Jesus Christ, of Latter Day Saints in Missouri," 148; also in *JSP*, H2:148.

34. Eliza R. Snow, "The Slaughter on Shoal Creek, Caldwell County, Missouri," *Times and Seasons* 1, no. 2 (December 1839):32.

35. Sidney Rigdon, *An Appeal to the American People: Being an account of the persecutions of the Church of Latter Saints; and of the Barbarities inflicted on them by the Inhabitants of the State of Missouri. By Authority of Said Church* (Cincinnati: Glezen and Shepard, Stereotypers and Printers, 1840), 51.

36. "Horrors of the Missouri Democracy," *New York Spectator*, July 1, 1839, 4.

37. "Great Meeting in Behalf of Mormon Women and Children," *New York Morning Herald*, September 17, 1839, n. p.

38. *Deseret News*, April 24, 1854, n. p.

39. James Adams to Martin Van Buren, November 9, 1839, Van Buren Correspondence, CHL.

40. Joseph Smith and Elias Higbee to Hyrum Smith and the High Council, December 5, 1839, Letterbook 2:85, MS 155, bx 2, fd 2, CHL.

41. Joseph Smith, Sidney Rigdon, and Elias Higbee, January 27, 1840, Records of the United States Senate, 26th–28th Congress, RG 46, bx 91, National Archives, Washington, DC.

42. Senate Report, March 4, 1840, 26th Congress, 1st Session, *Congressional Globe*.

43. Elias Higbee, John Taylor, and Elias Smith, Second Memorial, January 10, 1842, Records of the United States Senate, 26th–28th Congress, RG 46, bx 99, National Archives, Washington, DC.

44. Church Historian's Office, Manuscript History of the Church, November 29, 1843, E–1, 1790, CR 100 102, CHL.

45. Benjamin Andrews, "An Appeal to the People of the State of Maine," *Nauvoo Neighbor*, January 17, 1844, 1; Phineas Richards, "An APPEAL to the INHABITANTS of Massachusetts," *Nauvoo Neighbor*, February 7, 1844; and Joseph Smith, Journal, November 30, 1843, and February 2, 1844, CHL.

46. Andrews, "An Appeal to the People of the State of Maine," 1.

47. Richards, "An APPEAL to the INHABITANTS of Massachusetts," 2.

48. Andrews, "An Appeal to the People of the State of Maine," 1.

49. Sidney Rigdon, "To the Honorable, the Senate and House of Representatives of Pennsylvania, in Legislative Capacity Assembled," *Nauvoo Neighbor*, January 31, 1844, 1.

50. "Memorial of the Members and Officers of the Legislative Assembly of the Territory of Utah, setting forth Their grievances, and praying Congress to give them a voice in the selection of their rulers," House of Representatives, 35th Congress, 1st Session, Misc. Doc. No. 100, printed March 17, 1858, PAM 12436, Utah State Historical Society, Salt Lake City (hereafter cited as USHS).

51. Brigham Young to Horace S. Eldredge, April 5, 1858, Brigham Young Papers, Correspondence Collection, MSS B–93, USHS.

52. "Memorial of the Members and Officers of the Legislative Assembly of the Territory of Utah," 4–5.

53. John Wolcott Phelps, Diary Book A, October 17, 1857, John Wolcott Phelps Papers, MSS B 120, bx 1, fd. 3, USHS.

54. "Memorial of the Members and Officers of the Legislative Assembly of the Territory of Utah," 4–5.

Mormon Victims and Survivors in the Hawn's Mill Massacre

KILLED

Hiram Abbot—Mortally wounded while trying to escape from the blacksmith shop. He was taken care of by David Lewis until his death five weeks later. He was not buried in the well where the fourteen other victims were interred.

Elias Benner—Killed in the blacksmith shop.

John Byers—Killed in the blacksmith shop.

Alexander Campbell—Killed in the blacksmith shop.

Simon Cox—Mortally wounded while in the blacksmith shop. He lived until the next day.

Josiah Fuller—Killed in the blacksmith shop. The Fuller family apparently did not remain with the Church following the Missouri episode. In 1887, Fuller's son, a resident of Adair County, Missouri, visited Hawn's Mill, where he and Charles R. Ross located the well site where fourteen of the victims were buried and marked it using one of the millstones.

Austin Hammer—Mortally wounded while defending the blacksmith shop. He and his family lived several miles from Hawn's Mill but he was guarding the site at the time of the attack. While wounded, he was dragged out of the blacksmith shop where his assailants stripped him of his boots. After the ordeal he was transported to Jacob Hawn's home where he died around midnight. He received seven bullets and both thighs were broken.

John Lee—Killed in the blacksmith shop.

Benjamin Lewis—Mortally wounded while trying to make his escape from the blacksmith shop. Benjamin's brother, David Lewis, found him and brought him back to his home, where he died a few hours later. He was not buried in the well along with the other victims. David buried him in a grave on his (David's) property. Sometime later, Benjamin's remains were exhumed and moved to a local cemetery.

Thomas McBride—Brutally mutilated and then killed by Jacob S. Rogers of Daviess County after escaping from the blacksmith shop. The McBrides lived about three-quarters of a mile from the mill. At age 62, he was the oldest of the Hawn's Mill victims.

Charles Merrick—Mormon boy, age nine, son of Levi and Philindia Merrick. He received three wounds while trying to escape from the blacksmith shop. He died four weeks later and was not buried in the well where the fourteen other victims were interred.

Levi N. Merrick—Killed in the blacksmith shop.

William Napier [Naper]—Killed in the blacksmith shop. He was shot in the head and the chest.

George S. Richards—Killed in the blacksmith shop. He was the fifteen-year-old son of Phineas and Wealthy Richards. It was reported he was shot in the head and died instantly.

Sardius Smith—Mormon boy, age ten, son of Warren and Amanda B. Smith. He went into the blacksmith shop at the time of the attack and hid behind the bellows. Upon being discovered, he was shot in the head and killed. There are conflicting reports